"Sea-ing/Seeing A Vision Beyond The Surface"

BRANDON T. MITCHELL

ISBN: 9798649953177

BRANDON T. MITCHELL

AN AGENDA TO EAT, PLAY & DIGEST

CHAPTER 1

ON-BRAND FOOD FOR THOUGHT STORIES, QUOTES AND POETRY

PART 1: ON-BRAND FOOD FOR THOUGHT STORIES AND POETRY

PART 2: ON-BRAND FOOD FOR THOUGHT QUOTES AND POETRY

CHAPTER 2

ON-BRAND PLAY ON WORD STORIES, QUOTES AND POETRY

PART 1: ON-BRAND PLAY ON WORD STORIES

PART 2: ON-BRAND PLAY ON WORD QUOTES AND POETRY

"Sea-ing/Seeing A Vision Beyond The Surface"

INTRO-VISION

The Public Eye of this Branded Work Of Art is taking 15 of my best stories from my 3rd book, "38 MAGNETS" and 51 of my best "ON-BRAND" Quotes from my 2nd book, "Words From The Wise To Enlighten One's Mind" and expounding, more comprehensively, on many of the stories and quotes. 51 + 15 = 66, and 66 is the symbol for universal love. In other words, there's plenty of love that was put into writing this book. In the Bible, the Old and New Testament book have 66 books in total.

Through the seasoning of addons, many of these stories and quotes have been flavored/favored, by God's Grace, as MASTERPIECES of HIS works operating through me.

> *Now ye are the body of Christ, and members in particular* ***(1 Corinthians 12:27)****. Ye are the salt of the earth: but if the salt have lost his savour, shall it be salted? it is thenceforth good for nothing, but to be cast out, and to be trodden under foot of men* ***(Matthew 5:13)****.*

The wisdom that the Lord has blessed me with is too much for me to hold to myself. Therefore, I have to release what God has given me, to share with others.

> *How much better is it to get wisdom than gold! and to get understanding rather to be chosen than silver* ***(Proverbs 16:16)****!*

The cover of both books are collaborated together, into one cover. In the equation below, I am not adding 2 + 3 = 5 as I would in regular mathematics. I rotated the design of my 3rd book (38 MAGNETS), clockwise 90 degrees, and placed the design, as glasses/binoculars, onto the sun. The glare from the glasses/binoculars going down into the water is showing a 20 in both glares, representing a 20/20 vision, along with the year 2020, when the book was published. Now, suppose you wish to critique me on my addition technique: If you add all 4 numbers together as 2 + 0 + 2 + 0, you will get 4. There you have it! Everything is adding up to my 4th book. Now, you can see, it all lines up.

BOOK 2 COVER + BOOK 3 COVER = BOOK 4 COVER

And ye shall know that I am in the midst of Israel, and that I am the LORD your God, and none else: and my people shall never be ashamed. And it shall come to pass afterward, that I will pour out my spirit upon all flesh; and your sons and your daughters shall see visions ***(Joel 2:27-28)****. Where there is no vision, the people perish: but he that keepeth the law, happy is he* ***(Proverbs 29:18)****. The LORD on high is mightier than the noise of many waters, yea, than the mighty waves of the sea* ***(Psalm 93:4)****.*

"Sea-ing/Seeing A Vision Beyond The Surface" are my own stories and quotes which God has given me, to share with others. They will have you thinking and laughing. The purpose for launching this book is for the vision, for people to see the ways of life from other perspectives, and how words and pictures, also, speak life. I added three frames to my photo, that was placed on the back cover of this book, with the Synopsis. That will give the frame a 3D appearance and the impression of a vibration. This image is called: Vibrating in The Frame Of Mind/Mine. The Frame of Mind in this scenario is a mind-set or outlook on a positive reflection. The Frame of Mine is the frame in which I created for my photo, with my imagination and the meaning behind this creation. The reason for vibrations in the framework is to manifest the thoughts that God has blessed me with, as being electrifying food for the soul, or perhaps, shocking statements.

After reading each short story and each quote, my motive is for the scholars to become enrichened with wisdom and to have a great time being educated. As a car comes with a key to operate, God has blessed me with the key to a Porsche (portion) of HIS wisdom, to give me drive, so that I will share HIS wisdom with others. Each story goes into PACIFIC/specific detail to help scholars SEA/see a vision beyond the surface. That there is much to learn from each story and quote, and as I have [also] put in a lot of HEART work, this book was created with lots of class.

Wisdom is the principal thing; therefore get wisdom: and with all thy getting get understanding ***(Proverbs 4:7)****.*

ACKNOWLEDGEMENT

This book is dedicated to my God. It is He who has given me the inspiration to write this book. It allows individuals who read this book to speak, think, laugh, and live a more positive life style.

CHAPTER 1

"ON-BRAND FOOD FOR THOUGHT STORIES/QUOTES AND POETRY"

PART 1:

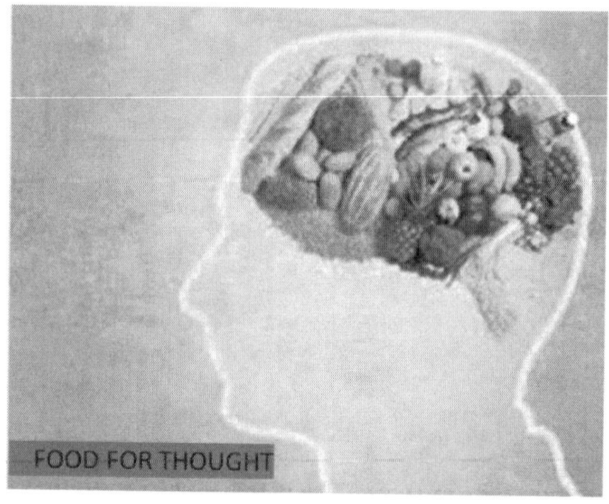

ON-BRAND FOOD FOR THOUGHT STORIES AND POETRY

"Seeing Past The Seashore"

A vision will come through a see/sea. That water has a reflection, perhaps it was created for a see/sea of beauty.

But, if you can get over the sees/seas of this world, then you can walk by faith, and not by sight. Isn't most of this world surrounded by the waters? If you go by a see/sea, a see/sea will only go so far. But, if you go by faith, you will go farther than a see/sea. If you put your faith in God, for His will in your life, He will take you farther than you can see/sea. God will take you over-sees/overseas.

> *Then thou shalt see, and flow together, and thine heart shall fear, and be enlarged; because the abundance of the sea shall be converted unto thee, the forces of the Gentiles shall come unto thee* ***(Isaiah 60:5)***.

Therefore, by God's will, you can overcome your mind, to not be drowned in your own thoughts. If you can't come up higher in the Lord, then do you have the faith to walk across the waters on your own, or does your eyes take away your faith, to walk over a see/sea?

> *So when they had rowed about five and twenty or thirty furlongs, they see Jesus walking on the sea, and drawing nigh unto the ship: and they were afraid **(John 6:19)**.*

If you walk by sight, and not by faith, then whose site will you walk on? Furthermore, whose side will you walk on, or which walk will you decide on?

ENTER YE IN AT THE STRAIT GATE: FOR WIDE IS THE GATE, AND BROAD IS THE WAY, THAT LEADETH TO DESTRUCTION, AND MANY THERE BE WHICH GO IN THEREAT (MATTHEW 7:13).

BECAUSE STRAIT IS THE GATE, AND NARROW IS THE WAY, WHICH LEADETH UNTO LIFE, AND FEW THERE BE THAT FIND IT (MATTHEW 7:14).

> *(For we walk by faith, not by sight:) We are confident, I say, and willing rather to be absent from the body, and to be present with the Lord. Wherefore we labour, that, whether present or absent, we may be accepted of him **(2 Corinthians 5:7-9)**.*

Will you be in a danger zone where there is destruction of a tearing down of a building, or are you walking by faith, to a building up of positive strongholds that can't be knocked down? In this scenario, positive strongholds are referred to as holding strong onto the Lord. But, if negative strongholds can add up, to make you stronger, then what is weighing you down?

> *Now faith is the substance of things hoped for, the evidence of things not seen **(Hebrews 11:1)**. While*

> *we look not at the things which are seen, but at the things which are not seen: for the things which are seen are temporal; but the things which are not seen are eternal* ***(2 Corinthians 4:18)****.*

To elaborate, if negative strongholds may add up, to be positive, then aren't we supposed to count the negatives in our lives as all joy? Don't give into a ragging pout about it to be a grouch about it. There are times that we have to keep a shut mouth about it. Just give God a praise shout about it. It will block all of the doubt about it, so that God will work in you, a new route out of it.

> *My brethren, count it all joy when ye fall into divers temptations; Knowing this, that the trying of your faith worketh patience* ***(James 1:2-3)****. Therefore I take pleasure in infirmities, in reproaches, in necessities, in persecutions, in distresses for Christ's sake: for when I am weak, then am I strong* ***(2 Corinthians 12:10)****.*

Moreover, when you walk by faith, and not by sight, you will have to recite what you want, by the power of your tongue. If you don't recite what you want by faith, you will continue to resight/recite/reside where you are and prolong your case.

> *And Jesus answering saith unto them, Have faith in God. For verily I say unto you, That whosoever shall say unto this mountain, Be thou removed, and be thou cast into the sea; and shall not doubt in his heart, but shall believe that those things which he saith shall come to pass; he shall have whatsoever he saith. Therefore I say unto you, What things soever ye desire, when ye pray, believe that ye receive them, and ye shall have them* ***(Mark 11:22-24)****.*

If you say, "I am going to go with God", then you are also saying, "I will go with God". Therefore, if God is "I Am", then shouldn't He be your will? You can overcome every obstacle in life, for every situation, as far, and as long as you can see/sea your way through Christ. If you have the ability to walk across the waters of a see/sea, without fear, as Peter once tried, and not be distracted by the winds, then you can go all the way with Christ the first time instead of making this a repeater's/re-Peter's course. Perhaps, because Peter did not pass the test, the grade of his name was shy of making the "a".

Peater lost his "a" and became **Peter.**

Isn't the far distance that you go with God also the long distance with God? For every circumstance that you will come to see/sea your way through, by the guidance of God, you can pass to walk assured/a shore.

> *And in the fourth watch of the night Jesus went unto them, walking on the sea. And when the disciples saw him walking on the sea, they were troubled, saying, It is a spirit; and they cried out for fear. But straightway Jesus spake unto them, saying, Be of good cheer; it is I; be not afraid. And Peter answered him and said, Lord, if it be thou, bid me come unto thee on the water. And he said, Come. And when Peter was come down out of the ship, he walked on the water, to go to Jesus. But when he saw the wind boisterous, he was afraid; and beginning to sink, he cried, saying, Lord, save me. And immediately Jesus stretched forth his hand, and caught him, and said unto him, O thou of little faith, wherefore didst thou doubt* ***(Matthew 14:25-31)****?*

"Celebrating A Broken Record"

It's funny how we celebrate an occasion for someone breaking a record in sports. But, why is it that we feel the need to celebrate over a broken record, versus celebrating over a stronger record that's harder to break? Are the athletes trying to beat their competitors until they break them, before they cross the finish line? That the challenger has a heart to compete, are you trying to break their heart, so that you can tape a recording of it, over and over?

> *Know ye not that they which run in a race run all, but one receiveth the prize? So run, that ye may obtain. And every man that striveth for the mastery is temperate in all things. Now they do it to obtain a corruptible crown; but we an incorruptible. I therefore so run, not as uncertainly; so fight I, not as one that beateth the air* ***(1 Corinthians 9:24-26)****: He shall break in pieces mighty men without number, and set others in their stead* ***(Job 34:24)****. But now they break down the carved work thereof at once with axes and hammers* ***(Psalm 74:6)****.*

Why break your brother's record that he worked so hard to pay the price for, instead of helping your brother in this race called life? If you take over the torch, by giving your brother a helping hand, you can both stay on track.

If breaking someone's best record sounds like music to your ears, then how would you like if someone had broken the record to your favorite hit song? Moreover, if your best record, that was broken, had your name and picture on it, will the pitch of your voice sing the same tune, after returning from a mournful seasonal

Break? Perhaps, your voice would become a broken oldie and dusty record.

> *The Jews therefore, because it was the preparation, that the bodies should not remain upon the cross on the sabbath day, (for that sabbath day was an high day,) besought Pilate that their legs might be broken, and that they might be taken away. Then came the soldiers, and brake the legs of the first, and of the other which was crucified with him. But, when they came to Jesus, and saw that he was dead already, they brake not his legs: But one of the soldiers with a spear pierced his side, and forthwith came there out blood and water. And he that saw it bare record, and his record is true: and he knoweth that he saith true, that ye might believe. For these things were done, that the scripture should be fulfilled, A BONE OF HIM SHALL NOT BE BROKEN* ***(John 19:31-36)***.

Looking from another perspective, many people have spoken the term, "I have a bone to pick with you." Does a person feel the need to pick a bone with someone, to get underneath their skin?

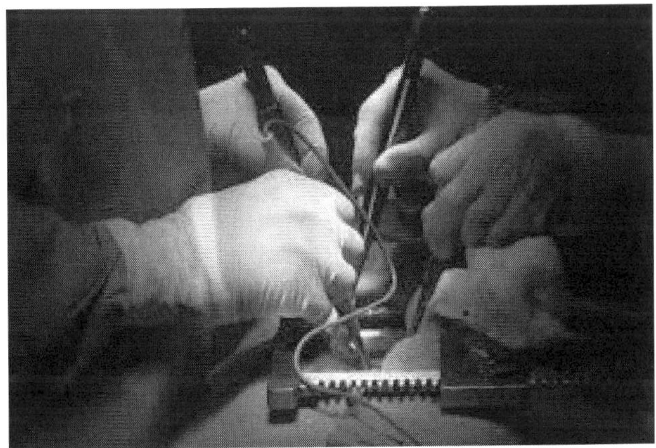

Is someone trying to skele/scale them down to grab the joy out of their heart until it is broken, or is the person trying to skull them down with the skill of mind games?

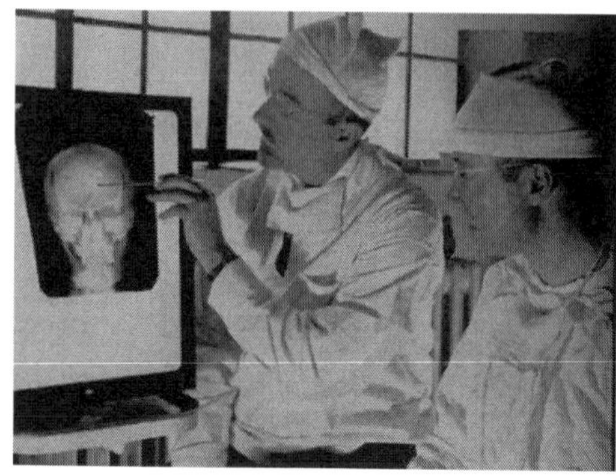

Maybe, he's just being a wise guy, or perhaps, a brainiac.

> *Make me to hear joy and gladness; that the bones which thou hast broken may rejoice. Hide thy face from my sins, and blot out all mine iniquities. Create in me a clean heart, O God; and renew a right spirit within me* ***(Psalms 51:8-10)****. By long forbearing is a prince persuaded, and a soft tongue breaketh the bone* ***(Proverbs 25:15).*** *Behold, my servants shall sing for joy of heart, but ye shall cry for sorrow of heart, and shall howl for vexation of spirit* ***(Isaiah 65:14).*** *A wise man scaleth the city of the mighty, and casteth down the strength of the confidence thereof* ***(Proverbs 21:22).***

Why is it that a person works so hard to break into someone's heart, or fraud into their mind, instead of helping that person to strengthen their heart, and encourage positive thoughts? Does a person find it a pleasure to reach for someone else's joy? Maybe, they want to see a mind destroyed, and a heart broken, as they do a record. Furthermore, why not plan on breaking Satan's record against us, since his plan is to break us from our livelihood? For the record, the adversary is our real enemy.

> *And whatsoever ye do, do it heartily, as to the Lord, and not unto men* ***(Colossians 3:23)****; But rejoice, inasmuch as ye are partakers of Christ's sufferings; that, when his glory shall be revealed, ye may be glad also with exceeding joy* ***(1 Peter 4:13)****. Be sober, be vigilant; because your adversary the devil, as a roaring lion, walketh about, seeking whom he may devour: Whom resist stedfast in the faith, knowing that the same afflictions are accomplished in your brethren that are in the world* ***(1 Peter 5:8-9)****.*

Breaking a person's record, seems to work hand in hand, with the reason that an athlete puts all of their heart and mind into it.

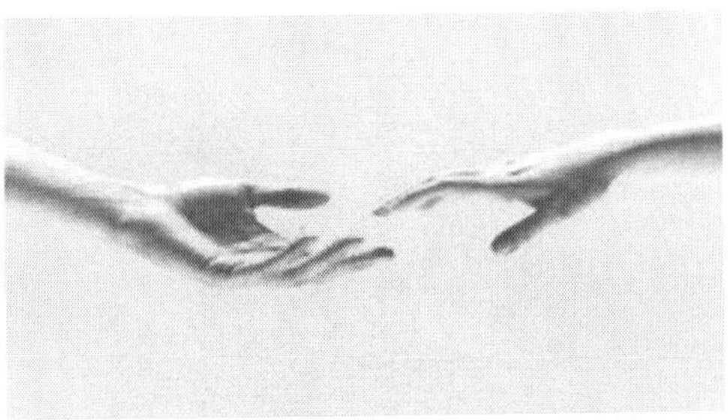

"MAN AND WOMAN"

Why separate with a torch when you can run in this life together, hand in hand? If two partners, on the same team, will keep hand in hand, then how can a heart be broken? Moreover, how can their record be broken if both partners are firm together as one whole/hold?

Is the heart and mind in good hands? Moreover, are the athletes putting all of their own hearts and minds into it, to reach for a goal/gold,

or do they have a mind to reach for someone else's heart in which they want to own? Maybe you are reaching for a broken record that's placed around a gold.

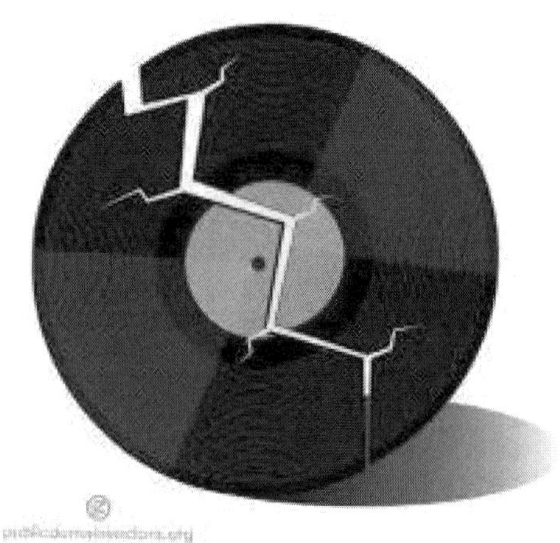

If someone medal's/meddles with you, and you see yourself as a gold, silver, or bronze, then who's there to steal/steel your joy, if your joy is in your heart? Moreover, if each part of your life is connected to a clip (as a part in a movie), then what is your life hooked on?

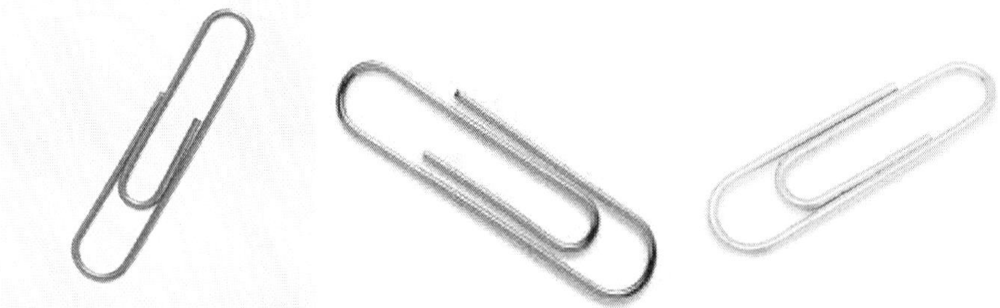

IS YOUR LIFE CLIPPED TO BRONZE, SILVER, OR GOLD MEMORIES? HOW DOES YOUR LIFE SHINE? MOREOVER, HOW DOES YOUR LIGHT SHINE ON OTHERS?

Is your life stable/stapled as firm as you would like it to be?

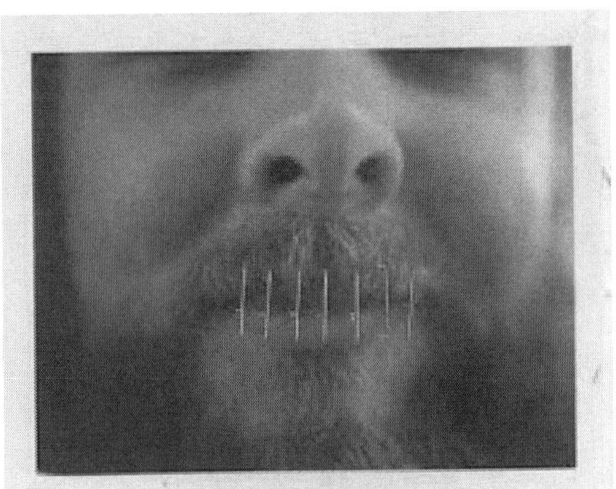

MANY TIMES SILENCE IS THE BEST OPTION TO KEEP YOUR LIFE FIRMLY STABLE/STAPLED, AS YOU ARE WHAT YOU SPEAK.

Furthermore, do you keep a record on file, in your mind, of bad things that have happened, or do you have those file/foul memories broken, for a breakthrough to joy? If you do keep a record in your mind, of things that have happened, then what does your mind record?

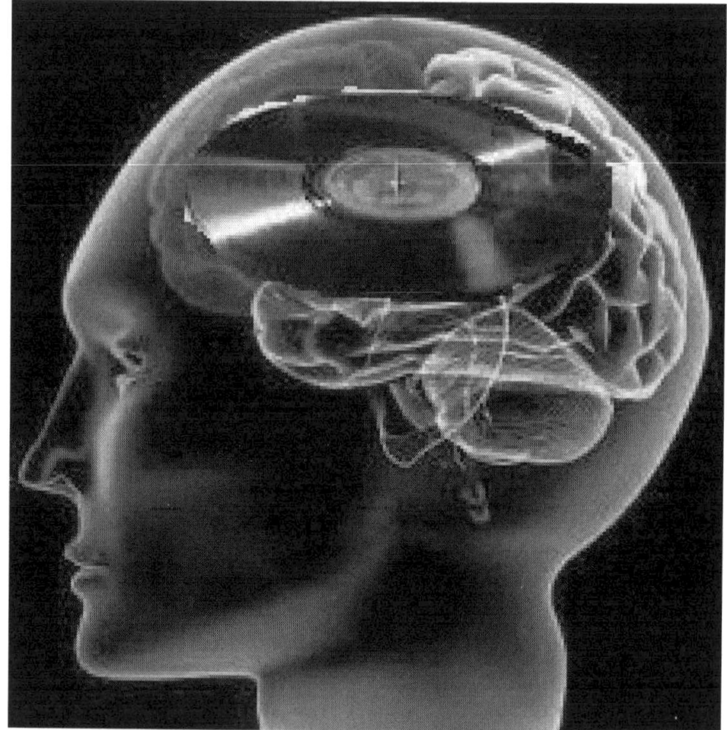

A RECORD THAT SKIPS TO PLAY OVER AND OVER, IN YOUR MIND, WILL CONTINUE AS A BROKEN RECORD. BUT, WITHOUT GOLDEN MEMORIES!

Let all bitterness, and wrath, and anger, and clamour, and evil speaking, be put away from you, with all malice: And be ye kind one to another, tenderhearted, forgiving one another, even as God for Christ's sake hath forgiven you ***(Ephesians 4:31-32)***.

"My Cell Phone Went Dead"

It's funny how people will say, "My cell phone went dead." Why is it that a person speaks death into a device that becomes useful at any given moment?

Death and life are in the power of the tongue: and they that love it shall eat the fruit thereof ***(Proverbs 18:21)***.

A cell phone works by juice, and juice is power. If a cell phone has no power, then it cannot function for another word to be spoken. It would have to be plugged in. But, doesn't a word have power?

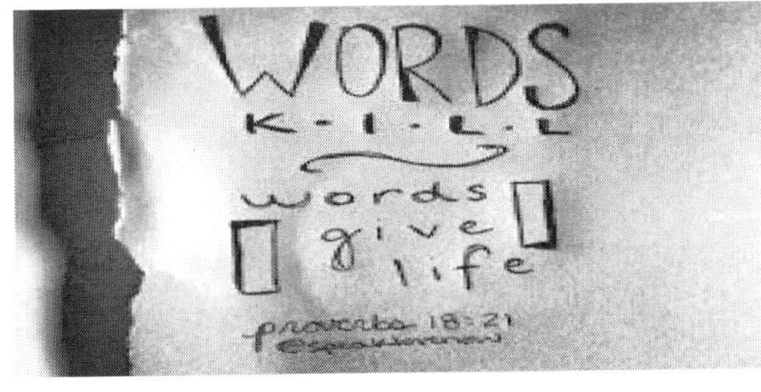

If we are not plugged into God's word, then how much power are we losing? Moreover, if we are not plugged into God's source of energy, then what source/sort/short of energy are we plugged into? Perhaps, there could be a power outage. Furthermore, as we speak with the members of our mouths, into a cell phone, isn't a cell phone losing its life, unless it is plugged in? Moreover, if God created us with cells to function, then why not call on Him to be charged, considering that He is the ultimate charger over us?

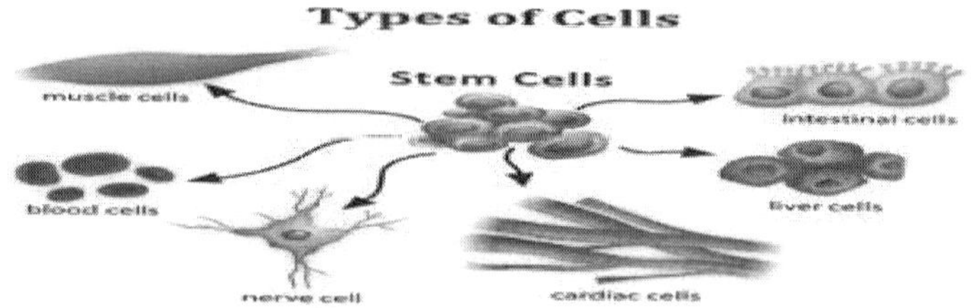

> *Even so the tongue is a little member, and boasteth great things. Behold, how great a matter a little fire kindleth! And the tongue is a fire, a world of iniquity: so is the tongue among our members, that it defileth the whole body, and setteth on fire the course of nature; and it is set on fire of hell* ***(James 3:5-6)****. He that keepeth his mouth keepeth his life: but he that openeth wide his lips shall have destruction* ***(Proverbs 13:3)****. Ever learning, and never able to come to the knowledge of the truth* ***(2 Timothy 3:7)****.*

If we have a better, stronger, and a more prosperous life than a cell phone, then how come a cell phone's reception have more word than each one of us? Does that sound like a sellout/cell out? A cell phone is more receptive to man's word, that is not always true, than man is accepting to God's word, that is truth in all ways. A cell phone will quote what a man or a woman would send through a text, more so than a person would quote God's word through trials and a test. In other words, a cell phone usually has no problem delivering a message by a man or a woman, but there are many times that the masters of cell phones will not submit to delivering God's word, who is our Master.

A man told me one day in a text message, "Please, forgive me for any misspelled words or incorrect grammar." This was sent to my cell phone. I replied in conversed words, "I won't hold you accountable for misspelled grammar. Neither will I hold your cell phone accountable for errors. If I held either one of our cell phones accountable for every mistake, then I may not have a call on my life.

> *"Be not thou therefore ashamed of the testimony of our Lord, nor of me his prisoner: but be thou partaker of the afflictions of the gospel according to the power of God; Who hath saved us, and called us with an holy calling, not according to our works, but according to his own purpose and grace, which was given us in Christ Jesus before the world began* ***(2 Timothy 1:8-9)****, For the gifts and calling of God are without repentance* ***(Romans 11:29)****.*

When two men are debating against each other, whether it's a friendly debate, or debating on harsh terms, they may speak with slang terminology. Mic may say to Will, "I don't think you have the juice to speak against me." Will would respond, "Where there's a will, there's a way." If juice is to power, then who has the most word to conquer victory, Will or Mic?

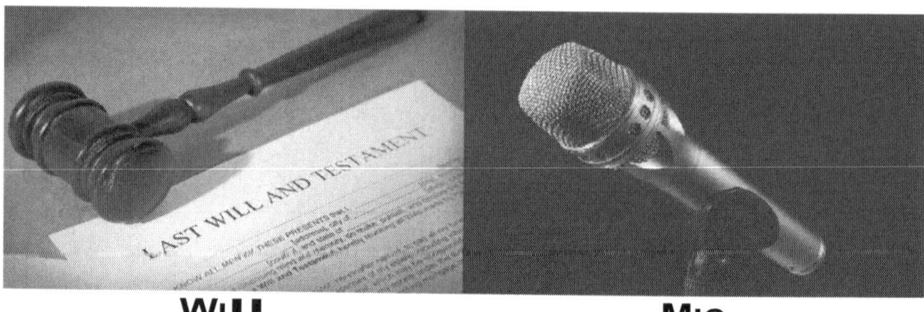

Will **Mic**

Will can turn a mic off, but Mic doesn't have the power to stop a will. A mic cannot speak by itself. Therefore, without a word, it has no power. Someone will have to speak up in its place/base. But, a will has the power of attorney, and it can speak for itself. We should have that same attitude for God's word. His word is our will. It is, also, our juice (as the fruit of the spirit), which is the power source for our energy, so that we will not go dead.

A will = Juice = Power

But, it never fells, many people wants to be like Mic. But, will Mic ever stand if it has no speaker? On that note, God's will stands forever.

> *Now unto him that is able to do exceeding abundantly above all that we ask or think, according to the power*

> *that worketh in us* ***(Ephesians 3:20)****, And he said unto me, My grace is sufficient for thee: for my strength is made perfect in weakness. Most gladly therefore will I rather glory in my infirmities, that the power of Christ may rest upon me* ***(2 Corinthians 12:9)****.*

If a cell phone is dead, it will be no longer useful. Speaking of a cell phone being so useful, to the point that we can't live without it, aren't the cells that we were created with more important? Keeping them functioning will maintain our lives. God has given each one of us the ability to charge and empower ourselves, through His word.

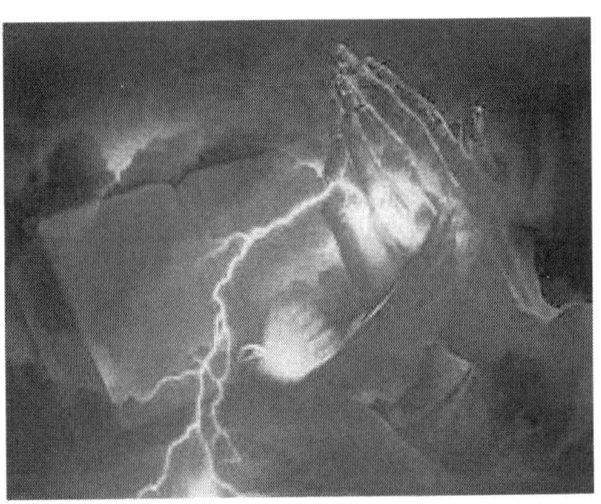

If we are prisoners of our cell phones, and the word of God is in each cell, then why not get lock into God's word for protection over our lives, and look for His call, for our purpose in Him? Moreover, we have the ability to charge and empower our lives through the cells of Jesus' blood.

> *According as his divine power hath given unto us all things that pertain unto life and godliness, through the knowledge of him that hath called us to glory and virtue*

> **(2 Peter 1:3)**: *For the life of the flesh is in the blood: and I have given it to you upon the altar to make an atonement for your souls: for it is the blood that maketh an atonement for the soul* **(Leviticus 17:11)**.

A cell phone connection to the internet is fed from Wi-Fi. But, isn't Wi-Fi and a cell phone created by man? Once again, aren't our blood cells created by God? If we were created by the same Father in Heaven, then why do we treat our cell phones with more value than our brothers and sisters in Christ?

A cell phone dressed in a tuxedo!

> *Who hath saved us, and called us with an holy calling, not according to our works, but according to his own purpose and grace, which was given us in Christ Jesus before the world began, But is now made manifest by the appearing of our Saviour Jesus Christ, who hath abolished death, and hath brought life and immortality to light through the gospel* **(2 Timothy 1:9-10)**:

When a person has a chip on their shoulder, don't they start acting up? When a cell phone has a built in chip, doesn't it get activated? When we have a chip on our shoulder, are we doing everything that we are supposed to do through our Lord? Perhaps, the chip on a person's shoulder may have too much salt, which may cause high blood pressure. On the other hand, when a FM radio chip is installed into a cell phone, to whom is a cell phone controlled by?

A. It's Master (you)
B. The Chip
C. Both

> *No man can serve two masters: for either he will hate the one, and love the other; or else he will hold to the one, and despise the other. Ye can not serve God and mammon* ***(Matthew 6:24)****. Take heed, brethren, lest there be in any of you an evil heart of unbelief, in departing from the living God. But exhort one another daily, while it is called To day; lest any of you be hardened through the deceitfulness of sin* ***(Hebrews 3:12-13)****.*

It's something how a cell phone device randomly calls any number it wants to call, while it is in your pocket, without your permission. Is it dialing numbers on its own, or does your pocket tell your cell phone who to call on? If your pocket has the keys to success, then just maybe, your cell phone is controlled by the keys of your pocket. Perhaps, a cell phone would take a photo of all your business, and its trace would be right on the money. Therefore, I would be sure to keep it away from my wallet. If we have a better life than a cell phone device, then how come we are not controlled by the keys of God's word, which is the entrance/interest to His kingdom? Now, because His word is rich, isn't that how we gain a wealthy living as a Prophet/profit? A cell phone device will make many false calls that we may bet our lives on. But, with God, He has a true calling for each one of our lives, that we can live on. God's call for our lives is no mistake. Why do we doubt Him?

> *When he shall come to be glorified in his saints, and to be admired in all them that believe (because our testimony among you was believed) in that day. Wherefore also we pray always for you, that our God would count you worthy of this calling, and fulfil all the good pleasure of his goodness, and the work of faith with power: That the name of our Lord Jesus Christ may be glorified in you, and ye in him, according to the grace of our God and the Lord Jesus Christ* ***(2 Thessalonians 1:10-12)****. There is one body, and one Spirit, even as ye are called in one hope of your calling; One Lord, one faith, one baptism, One God and Father of all, who is above all, and through all, and in you all* ***(Ephesians 4:4-6)****, There are many devices in a man's heart; nevertheless the counsel of the LORD, that shall stand* ***(Proverbs 19:21)****. That your faith should not stand in the wisdom of men, but in the power of God* ***(1 Corinthians 2:5)****. Jesus answered, Verily, verily, I say unto thee, Except a man be born of water and of the Spirit, he cannot enter into the kingdom of God* ***(John 3:5)****.*

It's funny that a person would say, "I feel naked without my cell phone." How can a small device give any person that much coverage? Will we feel left out in the cold if we left our cell phones at home? Does Satan have the cell of your mind on every page, and every thought that is paged to you on your cell phone?

Perhaps, we will miss out on a hot message that would have gotten us heated or fired up.

"A SMOKING HOT MESSAGE"

Therefore, we would go home to get our cell phone devices to feel covered in a hot mess (hot message). But, why is it that when we forget our Bibles, we keep going when we know that God has a call for each one of us, that's not through a cell/sell/sale? But, if we are sold out for God, then our lives will sail smooth.

> *There is one body, and one Spirit, even as ye are called in one hope of your calling* ***(Ephesians 4:4)****;*

Will not He keep us covered and protected? A cell phone can fit into your hand and pocket. But, we can fit into the grace of God's right hand, and be left covered in His other hand, but never left alone.

> *Thou art my hiding place and my shield: I hope in thy word* ***(Psalm 119:114)****. Even there shall thy hand lead me, and thy right hand shall hold me* ***(Psalm 139:10)****.*

Moreover, a cell phone will run out of power, and will need to be charged, but God is always on charge for us. Even when we're asleep, He never runs out of power.

> *And what is the exceeding greatness of his power to usward who believe, according to the working of his mighty power, Which he wrought in Christ, when he raised him from the dead, and set him at his own right hand in the heavenly places, Far above all principality, and power, and might, and dominion, and every name that is named, not only in this world, but also in that which is to come* ***(Ephesians 1:19-21)****:*

On the other hand, there are more people using their cell phones to key in the scripture readings, during Church Service or Bible Study. If a cell phone is dropped into water, then it will be dead, because the cell phone will no longer be useful. But, when we are dropped into the water, through Jesus Christ, we are born again.

And now why tarriest thou? arise, and be baptized, and wash away thy sins, calling on the name of the Lord ***(Acts 22:16)****.*

That God's word is incorporated into a cell phone, how far will a phone sail, if it is powered up through the word of God? Furthermore, how far will God take us, through a cell phone, for the call He has on our lives?

> *But Jesus beheld them, and said unto them, With men this is impossible; but with God all things are possible* ***(Matthew 19:26)****. And ye are complete in him, which is the head of all principality and power: In whom also ye are circumcised with the circumcision made without hands, in putting off the body of the sins of the flesh by the circumcision of Christ: Buried with him in baptism, wherein also ye are risen with him through the faith of the operation of God, who hath raised him from the dead* ***(Colossians 2:10-12)****.*

"Son-Of-A-Gun vs Son-Of-God"

It's something how people speak the term, "You son-of-a-gun" with exceeding joy. But, we very seldom speak in terms, "Son-of-God!" But, isn't a gun a deadly weapon, and "Son-of-God" a lively weapon, who gives us exceeding joy? We also speak the phrase, "You're killin' me," when we hear someone tell a really funny joke. But, isn't laughter medicine which gives us exceeding joy? We also speak that same phase out of anger or impatience. If your actions are what you speak, then perhaps, is that one of the major reasons that people commit suicide? Furthermore, why TRI-umph over a lethal weapon, when you can TRI God's legal weapon (The Word of God), and be safe?

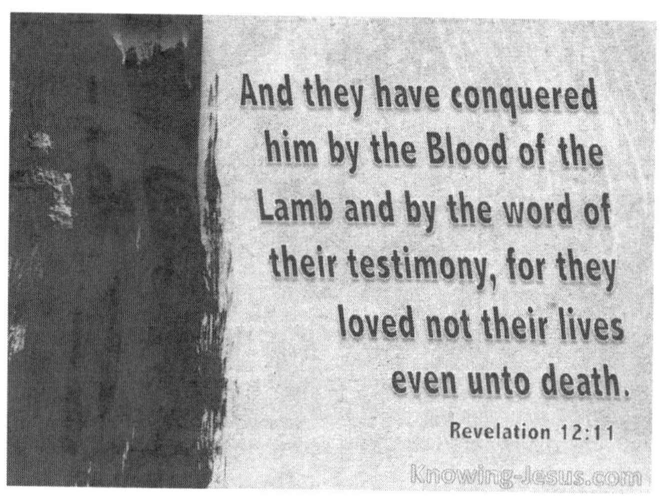

Moreover, doesn't God have power over any gun? With God, you have a better shot in life.

> *Behold, I have created the smith that bloweth the coals in the fire, and that bringeth forth an instrument for his work; and I have created the waster to destroy. No weapon that is formed against thee shall prosper; and every tongue that shall rise against thee in judgment thou shalt condemn. This is the heritage of the servants of the LORD, and their righteousness is of me, saith the LORD* ***(Isaiah 54:16-17)****.*

Would you rather shoot a gun or give a shout to God? With a gun that's made of man, you have the power in your hand to make a straight shot. But, with God, who made man, will give you power over all weapons that are formed against you. If you give a shout to God, He will keep you straight on target.

> *As newborn babes, desire the sincere milk of the word, that ye may grow thereby: If so be ye have tasted that the Lord is gracious. To whom coming, as unto a living stone, disallowed indeed of men, but chosen of God, and precious, Ye also, as lively stones, are built up a spiritual house, an holy priesthood, to offer up spiritual sacrifices, acceptable to God by Jesus Christ. Wherefore also it is contained in scripture, BEHOLD, I LAY IN SION A CHIEF CORNER STONE, ELECT, PRECIOUS: AND HE THAT BELIEVETH ON HIM SHALL NOT BE CONFOUNDED. Unto you therefore which believe he is precious: but unto them which be disobedient, THE STONE WHICH THE BUILDERS DISALLOWED, THE SAME IS MADE THE HEAD OF THE CORNER* ***(1 Peter 2:2-7)****,*

If you can literally stick a gun inside the volume of the Bible, being that the Bible is not condensed in size, then wouldn't the Word of the Lord give coverage to a 38 magnum? In addition, there is no need to page for anyone else, over a speaker (intercom) for help, when God is our #1 speaker who give us all the pages that we need for life, through His Word.

If that is the case in which it can hold that weapon, then why trust in something that's smaller than the word of God, to have protection over your life? A Bible can fit into your hand, and you can carry it around in a case, everywhere you go. But, if you take page by page of the wisdom of God, and build on that, wouldn't His word cover you as a tent? Therefore, as long as you will stay in the word of God, His word will have you covered, by His will.

Moreover, wouldn't you rather be covered in the will of God, to stay protected in a case full of instructions that's full of wisdom and power, than to take your chances on a cold case where you may suffer defeat? God's word is not for "Just in case", because it is for every case of our lives.

> *It is better to trust in the LORD than to put confidence in man* ***(Psalm 118:8)****.*

Furthermore, if you can place a gun inside the Bible, then whose volume is the loudest, that will give you the most fear?

> *And fear not them which kill the body, but are not able to kill the soul: but rather fear him which is able to destroy both soul and body in hell* ***(Matthew 10:28)****.*

Additionally, would you rather approach the son of someone pointing a gun to your head, or would you prefer to approach the Son-of-God, to make Him your head, to point you in the right direction, from all harm?

> *And who is he that will harm you, if ye be followers of that which is good* ***(1 Peter 3:13)****?*

A son-of-a-gun may miss the point, and target someone else's blood to take their life. The point in which they were directed, by their main/man head leader was misunderstood and they took the wrong blood. But, with the Son-of-God, Jesus' blood hits right on point, and targets to save your life. Consequently, Jesus' target is right on point, and His point is right on target. Furthermore, would you rather have a gun drawn for your blood, or would you prefer Jesus' blood drawn, in written formation, to guide you through life?

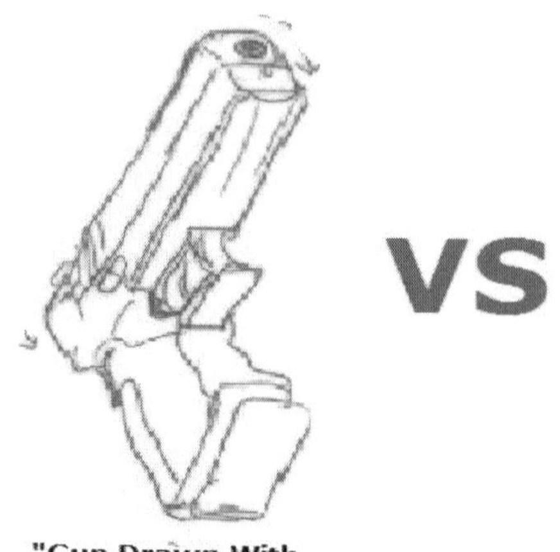

"Gun Drawn With Your Blood"

ST. JOHN, 4 The miss

should not perish, but have eternal life.
16 ¶ For God so loved the world, that
he gave his only begotten Son, that
whosoever believeth in him should not
perish, but have everlasting life.
17 For God sent not his Son into the
world to condemn the world; but that
the world through him might be saved.
18 ¶ He that believeth on him is not
condemned: but he that believeth not is
condemned already, because he hath not
believed in the name of the only begotten
Son of God.
19 And this is the condemnation, that
light is come into the world, and men
loved darkness rather than light, because
their deeds were evil.
20 For every one that doeth evil hateth
the light, neither cometh to the light,
lest his deeds should be reproved.
21 But he that doeth truth cometh to
the light, that his deeds may be made
manifest, that they are wrought in God.

"Jesus' Blood Written For Your Life"

"A leTHAl weAPOn cAUSes STRIfe, BUt THe WoRD Of GoD GIVes yoU LIFE!"

God made man. Therefore, He has control over man. That a gun is made by man, a man has jurisdiction over a gun. Therefore, why put your trust in something that you have power over, instead of putting your trust in God, who created you under His power? If you had a choice to be with a son-of-a-gun or the Son-Of-God, whose sentence would you rather be covered in for life?

> *But we had the sentences of death in ourselves, that we should not trust in ourselves, but in God which raiseth the dead: Who delivered us from so great a death, and doth deliver: in whom we trust that he will yet deliver us* ***(2 Corinthians 1:9-10)****;*

Moreover, whose tent/tense are you under? Why not trust in God to give you a twist of English to your life story by your faith in Him?

> *Then a cloud covered the tent of the congregation, and the glory of the LORD filled the tabernacle* ***(Exodus 40:34)****.*

THeRe ARe 3 MAIN VeRb Tense/Tents:

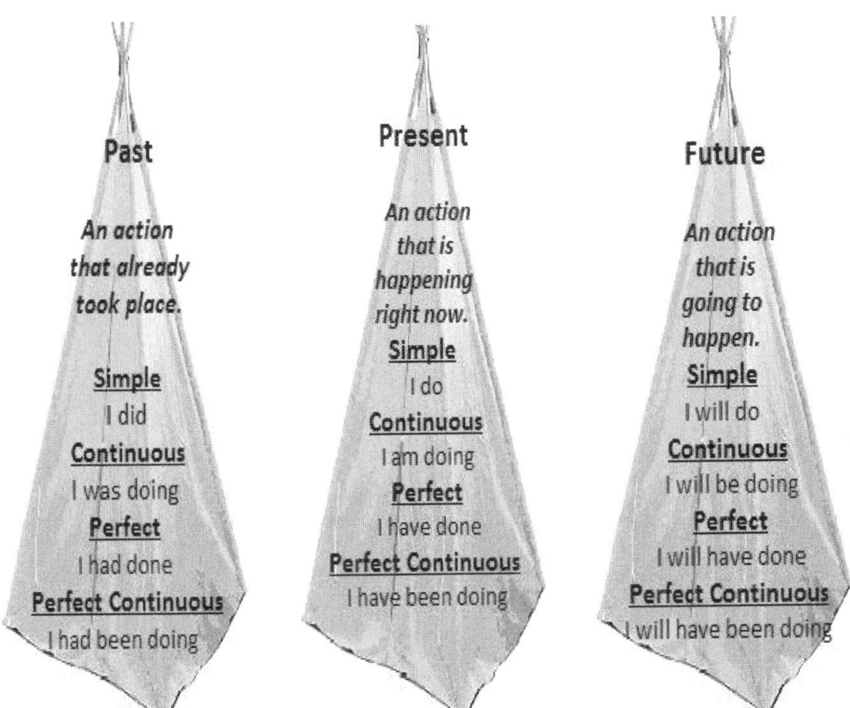

If you WeRe twisteD by youR PAST, THen HOW WOUlD you PRESENT youRSelf In THe now, to PReDICt youR FUTURE?

What skeletons are in your closet? Furthermore, what skeletons are in your tents/tense? In other words, do you ponder over memories of the *past*, or do you focus on the *present* to predict your *future*? Perhaps, if you focus on the *present*, the gift will come to you. What tent/tense are you sentenced under for life? If you are in the *past* tense/*past* tent, what you had should stay in the past, in order for you to pass the test, and not tense up on bad memories. If you are in the *future* tense/*future* tent, what you will have, is for you to have at God's will.

If you are in the *present* tense/*present* tent, the moment that you are having now, is a present for every moment that you are alive. It will affect your *future* for every tense/tenth of a second. After all is said, would you rather be sentenced as a prisoner to life for being with the Son of God, or sentenced for life, as a prisoner, for being with a son of a gun?

> *Now unto him that is able to keep you from falling, and to present you faultless before the presence of his glory with exceeding joy. To the only wise God our Saviour, be glory and majesty, dominion and power, both now and ever. A-men'* ***(Jude 1:24-25)***.

"From Funny Money To Rich Wisdom"

I approached a man one afternoon, as he was going into the trunk of his car.

I said: Hello Sir! Do you support entrepreneurs that are working toward a positive cause?

He replied: Yes, I do, at times when I can. What do you have?

I stated: I wrote a book.

He replied: Really? What is your book about?

I let him browse through the book, and I shared one of my poems as he was following along.

He said: Now, you quoted that word from word. You sold me on that one. Aww man, I wish that I could purchase your book, but right now, my money's funny!

I replied: Really Sir? You know what? The jokes in my book are funny too. Why not do a trade for a trade? Wait a minute. Before we do that, you said that your money is funny? That doesn't make it counterfeit does it?

He said: No, it doesn't make it counterfeit (As he laughs).

I replied: Ok then, I tell you what, I'll trade you the funny book for the funny money. Since your money's so funny, I'll laugh it right on to the bank, deposit it, and change it from funny to funding, and guess what?

He said: What?

I replied: The deposit won't take the fun out of it.

He said: Aww man, I never heard it like that before.

I replied: Me neither Sir! The Lord just gave it to me like that.

Even though he didn't purchase my book with his funny money, I'm sure that I left him with something to think about.

I've heard the expression, "Time is money!" If your currency may depreciate over time, then how do you speak about your wealth at the current time of depreciation? Do you speak positive energy or negative energy? Perhaps, if you speak negative about your cash flow, then you are speaking depreciation into your bank account.

> *But I say unto you, That every idle word that men shall speak, they shall give account thereof in the day of judgment. For by thy words thou shalt be justified, and by thy words thou shalt be condemned* ***(Matthew 12:36-37)****.*

It's hilarious how someone would say, "Put your money where your mouth is!" If a person makes this statement, to bet another man's/woman's money, means that they disagree with what comes out of their mouth, for it to be a negative. Therefore, if you disapprove of what comes out of another person's mouth, and you won the bet, then why take someone else's money where their mouth has been?

"PUT YOUR MONEY WHERE YOUR MOUTH IS"

Perhaps, you will walk around with a contagious disagreement, or an infectious negative agreement until you get rid of the liquid assets.

"LIQUID ASSETS DRIPPING AWAY"

Furthermore, why would you walk around with the proceeds from someone's mouth who is all talk, but no truth, and whom you never believed in the first place, for the reason that you bet them? Their proceeds will rub off on you. Perhaps, you will walk around with their false belief, or doubt. Then, how can you proceed in life for yourself, by faith, if you gain the proceeds of someone else, whom you have no trust? Maybe their proceeds would come out counterfeit. If so, then you will have an added fit to your worries. Moreover, that false money is bad business, then their liquid assets will turn your business into a liquidation.

Instead of taking your winnings from a person's mouth, to take a chance for your fingers to be chewed out as a bit-coin, which is a bit extreme, I'd rather take money from an ATM machine that gives me a receipt in return. I have no idea why anyone would take proceeds from a person's mouth in the 1st Place. Perhaps, their 2nd Place choice would not stand a chance. A person's word of mouth is like a word that is blown by the wind and lost in the air. Therefore, we have no way of finding a trace, because a "Word of Mouth" has no foundation on which it travels. It is not grounded, so then, how will it stand?

> *Set a watch, O LORD, before my mouth; keep the door of my lips* ***(Psalm 141:3)****. He that hath knowledge spareth his words: and a man of understanding is of an excellent spirit* ***(Proverbs 17:27)****. He becometh poor that dealeth with a slack hand: but the hand of the diligent maketh rich* ***(Proverbs 10:4)****. Let no corrupt communication proceed out of your mouth, but that which is good to the use of edifying, that it may minister grace unto the hearers* ***(Ephesians 4:29)****.*

I've heard the term, "Money talks!"

$MONEY TALKS$

If you put your money in a check, then doesn't it give you a financial statement? But, our mouths also make statements. There are times that it pays to put ourselves in check, by the words which we speak. If we don't, it may cost us.

DO YOU PUT YOURSELF IN CHECK? PERHAPS, IF WE CONCENTRATE ON PUTTING OURSELVES IN CHECK, INSTEAD OF PUTTING OTHERS IN CHECK, WE WILL MAKE OURSELVES RICH FOR THE STATEMENTS THAT WE'VE SAVED OVER TIME.

Either make the tree good, and his fruit good; or else make the tree corrupt, and his fruit corrupt: for the tree is known by his fruit. O generation of vipers, how can ye, being evil, speak good things? for out of the abundance of the heart the mouth speaketh. A good man out of the good treasure of the heart bringeth forth good things: and an evil man out of the evil treasure bringeth forth evil things ***(Matthew 12:33-35)****.*

Therefore, if you tell someone to put their money where their mouth is, and you won the bet, why take money from a person, whose word of mouth is incorrect, for their statements to come back void? How can you bank on them? If you put your money with a trust account, then the bank will serve as a custodian, and a trustee will keep legal control of the proceeds in the account. The trustee can be an accountant, a lawyer, or a family member to take over someone else's assets to handle the funds and the payments better, such as property cost. Therefore, why would you bank on a bet that you may win, and take money from a mouth that you have no trust? Perhaps, you would walk away having a bad fit. But, if the statements that comes out from the person's mouth is not real, then you will walk away with a counterfeit. If that's the case, you will walk around with funny money that can't be replaced. Then, you may intend to counteract. On the contrary, if words can be twisted in confusion, by both parties, then perhaps, there would be strings attached in a tie.

STRINGS ATTACHED IN A TIE IS KNOT/NOT FOR GOOD.

Therefore, no one wins. Because it was a draw, both parties will have to erase what they've started, to commence again.

> *Labour not to be rich: cease from thine own wisdom. Wilt thou set thine eyes upon that which is not? for riches certainly make themselves wings; they fly away as an eagle toward heaven* ***(Proverbs 23:4-5)****.*

Here's another scenario, where I approached a woman at a grocery store one morning.

I said: Hi Ma'am, do you support entrepreneurs that are executing a fundraiser toward a positive cause?

She stated: At times when I can, but not today.

I responded: Ok then, what time shall we meet on the following day?

She replied: Well, let me put it this-a-way, "I have a really busy calendar.

I rebutted: Really Madam? You know what? My calendar is really busy too. Every time I checked on it, my calendar was full of numbers, scheduled for its next date. My calendar is a real flirt. Everyday it is shining with the sun, and later on, it's moonlighting on the nightshift. As a matter of fact, my calendar is very romantic, because it goes out every single night, as it twinkles with the Stars/Starrs and goes Skyping along the way. It even gets flirtatious on Sundays.

At 11:59 PM, My Calendar Is About To Go Out And Get Fresh With A New Date.

December and January are really compatible for each other. To be so far apart, they stay connected to one another. That's because they have each other's numbers,

DECEMBER 2019						
SUN	MON	TUE	WED	THU	FRI	SAT
1	2	3	4	5	6	7
8	9	10	11	12	13	14
15	16	17	18	19	20	21
22	23	24	25	26	27	28
29	30	31				

JANUARY 2020						
SUN	MON	TUE	WED	THU	FRI	SAT
			1	2	3	4
5	6	7	8	9	10	11
12	13	14	15	16	17	18
19	20	21	22	23	24	25
26	27	28	29	30	31	

Holidays and Observances: 1: New Year's Day, 20: Martin Luther King Jr. Day

so they stay in touch, as they both trust with each other. Even through their cold season, and their week moments (Sunday through Saturday), they are hot for each other. December has such Merry days when it is connected to January, as January feels so cool and refreshing, from the start.

"JANUARY'S FORCAST IS A COOL BREEZE"

JANUARY IS LOOKING REALLY COOL WITH HIS *BOW TIE*, AS HE WHISTLE'S A COOL TUNE. JANUARY SAID TO DECEMBER, "I AD-DRESS MYSELF TO LOOK REALLY COOL, BUT I'M REALLY HOT FOR YOU, AS MY EYES ARE *TIED* ON YOU, EVEN WHEN I *BOW*!"

There's no wonder why December would ask January, "Will you Merry with me?" January responds, "It will be my pleasure, as I will feel like a Newlywed in this next year." As opposites do attract, the last second of December and the first second of January both kiss on their dates together, as the world, also, celebrates with them, during their Anniversary. December and January does not think of their kiss, as only, for a second moment. Instead, they feel/fill their kiss into the next minute, into the next hour, into the next day, into the next month and, also, into the next year. Perhaps, they look forward to the second time around, as they both blend so well with each other, on their dates, in their seasoned taste of winter-fresh romance. December and January are best at showcasing/snow-casing with each other.

Let thy fountain be blessed: and rejoice with the wife of thy youth. Let her be as the loving hind and pleasant roe; let her breasts satisfy thee at all times; and be thou ravished always with her love ***(Proverbs 5:18-19)***.

ISN'T THAT TWO LIPS KISSING WITH THEIR HEARTS? THEY'RE RIGHT ON SCHEDULE.

Now, is that perfect timing for a kiss, or what? By the aftermath of this moment, December and January are not divided apart from their dates, because they are a part of each other. December and January may not always kiss into the next week, but there Lipton (Lip-ton) moment may be in the middle of the week, during their tea party. Nevertheless, just because their kiss may not be on the first second of a new week does not mean that their timing was off schedule. But, a kiss on their Anniversary has always been a strong DJ moment (December January moment) and not a beginning of a week moment, because the beginning of their loving pledg-ures/pleasures, as a week moment, is not their cup of tea. On that note, December and January mate together as two love birds on the nightshift, yet, their trust is not in the dark. They both enjoy that second moment with each other, during their month to month resuscitation. There's a saying, "Time is money", and it is good to be on time. December and January come together with a kiss in that perfect second/perfect setting. Therefore, their kiss was right on time, and it was also, on the money. They are never late for their dates. Perhaps, they are both prompt material/prom material. As both December and January come together at first or at last, one month expresses its feelings to the other by stating, "Isn't it amazing how 'u'/you turned upside-down, at the 'n'/end, advances the course?"

IN "MOUTH" THE "U" UPSIDE-DOWN IS "N" AND IT BECOMES "MONTH". THE WORD "END" IN THE QUOTE ABOVE IS REFERRED TO AS THE BOTTOM.

It's difficult to tell who's giving and who's receiving, when they both trust together. Even through the storms that come between them, while January and December are so far apart from each other, they both manage to stay connected, because they never glance to the past, they keep moving forward. That's why we should kiss each date/day goodbye, and not look back. With that being said, my calendar is really busy too. It never has a dull moment. Perhaps, we can all learn about life from the dates of a calendar.

Isn't it amazing how the words that we speak, may change our lives? Let's look at the power of words from an algebraic perspective. As I will take the number two (2), and times (X) it to the 3rd power, I will retrieve this result:

$$2^3 = 2 \times 2 \times 2$$

$$= 4 \times 2$$

$$= 8$$

Now, with this same number (#2), I will use the "word power" in the place of the "3rd power". As there are four different letters in "word", I will employ the least whole number power for each letter. Therefore, w=1, o=2, r=3, and d=4.

2 TO THE "WORD POWER" IS WRITTEN AS: 2^{WORD}

with their respective numbers:

W X O X R X D =

1 X 2 X 3 X 4 = 24

Therefore, giving you 2 to the 24th power, written as:

$$2^{24} = 16{,}777{,}216$$

Wow! This is taking a small number (#2), as a mustard seed, and using the power of a positive word, to grow the mustard seed into a harvest.

> *It is like a grain of mustard seed, which, when it is sown in the earth, is less than all the seeds that be in the earth: But when it is sown, it groweth up, and becometh greater than all herbs, and shooteth out great branches; so that the fowls of the air may lodge under the shadow of it* ***(Mark 4:31-32)****. Blessed is the man that trusteth in the LORD, and whose hope the LORD is. For he shall be as a tree planted by the waters, and that spreadeth out her roots by the river, and shall not see when heat cometh, but her leaf shall be green; and shall not be careful in the year of drought, neither shall it cease from yielding fruit* ***(Jeremiah 17:7-8)****.*

Perhaps, you've heard the phrase, "One bad apple spoils the bunch!" Of all the positive letters in "word", if one of the members are negative, it will spoil it for the bunch. I will incorporate the least powered letter (w), to make it a negative one (-1), while the other letters will stay positive. As I bring up the same equation, I arrive to:

$$\text{w}=-1,\ \text{o}=2,\ \text{R}=3,\ \text{AND}\ \text{D}=4$$

$$2^{\text{WORD}} = 2^{(-1 \times 2 \times 3 \times 4)}$$

$$= 2^{-24}$$

$$= \frac{1}{16{,}777{,}216}.$$

It looks like, by the aftermath of the problem, from that one negative, or that negative one, everything that was built up over time, hide under the table. What happened to their trust, over that one negative? Isn't it something how one negative power seed can spoil it for the harvest? That's why we have to be careful with what we speak and choose our words wisely. A negative reward is from a negative drawer. Therefore, if you speak negatively, then you will draw negative, and receive negative.

REWARD IS DRAWER SPELLED BACKWARDS

Your glorying is not good. Know ye not that a little leaven leaveneth the whole lump? Purge out therefore the old leaven, that ye may be a new lump, as ye are unleavened. For even Christ our passover is sacrificed for us: Therefore let us keep the feast, not with old leaven, neither with the leaven of malice and wickedness; but with the unleavened bread of sincerity and truth ***(1 Corinthians 5:6-8)****.*

As words have power, then what power have you given money to move from you? Furthermore, do you budget your money, or does your money budge from you? If your money budges from you, then perhaps, that's why it runs out on you.

> *Let your conversation be without covetousness; and be content with such things as ye have: for he hath said, I WILL NEVER LEAVE THEE, NOR FORSAKE THEE* ***(Hebrews 13:5)****. For the love of money is the root of all evil: which while some coveted after, they have erred from the faith, and pierced themselves through with many sorrows. But thou, O man of God, flee these things; and follow after righteousness, godliness, faith, love, patience, meekness* ***(1 Timothy 6:10-11)****.*

That words are rich, then how valuable is each letter? If letters can merge together to form a word of power, then what strength do you have in a power statement. Moreover, if words can come together to form a statement of power, then how much more power will we have, if we come 2 or 3 gathered together, in agreement, to a form room, by prayer? A prayer can build to structure paragraphs/pair-of-graphs. Therefore, paragraphs/pair-of-graphs can draw pictures, and each picture is worth a thousand words, and a thousand words can form a great size letter. Perhaps, are letters called letters because, by the words that we speak or listen to, we letter (let it) happen to ourselves?

DEAR LORD,

NOW, AT THE END OF WRITING ALL OF YOUR LETTERS, PERHAPS, YOU WILL CATCH SOME ZZZZS!

Who also hath made us able ministers of the new testament; not of the letter, but of the spirit: for the letter killeth, but the spirit giveth life ***(2 Corinthians 3:6)****. Again I say unto you, That if two of you shall agree on earth as touching any thing that they shall ask, it shall be done for them of my Father which is in heaven. For where two or three are gathered together in my name, there am I in the midst of them* ***(Matthew 18:19-20)****.*

"A Kodak Moment vs A Show That-Moment"

It has been said, "A picture is worth a thousand words." On the contrary, it has also been said, "Actions speaks louder than words." But, do actions speak louder words?

- A Kodak moment is a picture taken.

- A show is a picture in action.

If a picture is worth a thousand words, then I wonder how many words can you summarize through your actions? If you go to the movies to see a picture in action, how will that picture move you? Then, after what you've learned, how would you act? With that being said, do your thoughts keep you in bondage?

For ye have not received the spirit of bondage again to fear; but ye have received the Spirit of adoption, whereby we cry, Ab'-ba, Father ***(Romans 8:15)****. And deliver them who through fear of death were all their lifetime subject to bondage* ***(Hebrews 2:15)****.*

If the thoughts of your mind were caught on camera, how many sentences will you have in your story?

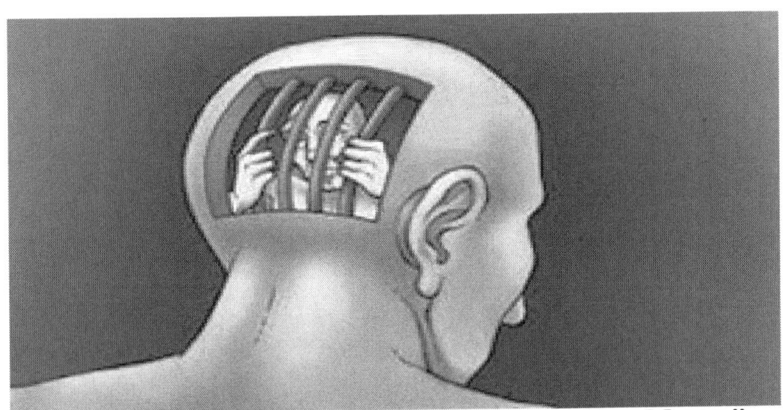

**"IN THE PRISON SENTENCE OF HIS MIND"
PERHAPS, HE'S IN THE TOP STORY OF HIS MIND, LOOKING DOWN IN DISAPPOINTMENT, AS HE HAVE MADE THE HEADLINES.**

Moreover, how many sentences would you have in a lifetime? Furthermore, if the thinking of a person's mind were to be captured on film, how many stories would there be in each prison, and how many life sentences would be on each story? If you were a judge that made one mistake in a sentence to a paragraph, that error may cause a person a life sentence in prison, that have only taken you a few minutes to write/right. But instead, you would have wronged them through a trial and error.

> *Speak not evil one of another, brethren. He that speaketh evil of his brother, and judgeth his brother, speaketh evil of the law: but if thou judge the law, thou art not a doer of the law, but a judge. There is one lawgiver, who is able to save and to destroy: who art thou that judgest another* ***(James 4:11-12)****?*

Words are powerful, as you have to, not only, watch what you speak, but you have to, also, be careful with what you speak,

"IF YOU CAN'T WATCH WHAT YOU SPEAK, THEN CAN YOU REALLY SEE WHAT YOU'RE SAYING YOURSELF? IF NOT, THEN YOU ARE BLIND TO YOUR OWN WORDS."

because a sentence and a statement can work hand and hand. If you say or give the wrong statement, isn't it amazing how that may cause you to be sentenced? On the flip side, if you said the wrong sentence, then the statement in which you bank on, may come back void. Moreover, each letter of the alphabets is called a character. If your name is who you are, and there was a movie that tells your life story, then how many characters are in the movie, to play a part to act as U (you), being only one character? If BRANDON has seven characters to play a part in his name, and one character, being absent, would not manifest the movie's full potential, then perhaps, BRANDON is a supercharacter from birth.

> *For the word of God is quick, and powerful, and sharper than any twoedged sword, piercing even to the dividing asunder of soul and spirit, and of the joints and marrow, and is a discerner of the thoughts and intents of the heart* ***(Hebrews 4:12)****. For HE THAT WILL LOVE LIFE, AND SEE GOOD DAYS, LET HIM REFRAIN HIS TONGUE FROM EVIL, AND HIS LIPS THAT THEY SPEAK NO GUILE* ***(1 Peter 3:10)****:*

If you were sentenced for life, then what state of mind were you in, and to speak on the power of words, what statement got you there? If you are freed from the prison of your mind, then you can make state-of-the-art decisions. Moreover, can you Art like The Lord? Perhaps, you can draw freehanded, and not be handcuffed and locked into your own thoughts, if they are the wrong thoughts. More less, why would you be locked into someone else's thoughts, for another person to take control over your life? Perhaps, you would not mind them to act for your decisions. With that being a two-way statement in the negative, your mind would lose either way. How can you make a great statement for yourself, if you are in a state of mind, other than your own? If you are in the sentence of another person's story, then how were you sent/sentenced there? The life of someone's story can be the prison of another person's mind.

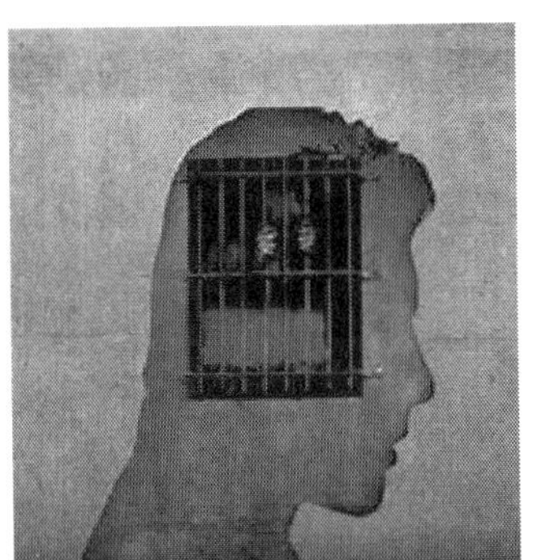

PERHAPS, HE'S IN THE PENTHOUSE/PINNED-HOUSE OF SOMEONE ELSE'S TOP STORY, AS HE IS PENT-UP OR PINNED DOWN IN MISERY, WRESTLING WITH HIS THOUGHTS OR STUCK IN THE MIND OF SOMEONE ELSE.

Therefore, you would have to pray, and ask Jehovah to direct your thoughts, because He is the leader of all leaders that will not guide you wrong. Why would anyone sit on another person's sentence if they can make a statement for themselves, to empower their own life?

> *But be ye doers of the word, and not hearers only, deceiving your own selves* ***(James 1:22)****. Even so faith, if it hath not works, is dead, being alone* ***(James 2:17)****.*

A Kodak moment is a picture taken at a particular time, but that photo may paint the wrong image to another person's mind. A "Show-That-Moment" is a moving picture on film, of a person's life, or a make-believe story shown onstage, in action. It is obvious, in this passage, actions speak louder than words. Now, in looking from a different perspective, let's take a cat walking behind you, during the moment you were writing about "The Cat's Silent Footsteps". The sound of the words being written on paper will be louder than the actions of the roaming cat. Perhaps, that's because your writings are your voice.

A Kodak moment is a flash shot, and a "Show-That-Moment" can be a flashback of memories.

FLASH SHOT

FLASHBACK

Would you rather have a flashback of your life, or a flash shot to new beginnings? A flashback will take you to the past, but to have a shot in life, will give you the opportunity to flash as a star/Starr, to reach others, and help them shine.

> *Let your light so shine before men, that they may see your good works, and glorify your Father which is in heaven* ***(Matthew 5:16)****.*

Perhaps, you can be their flashlight, to help them see the way.

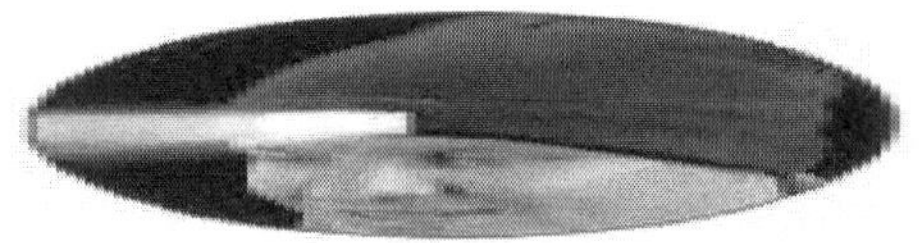

The right way may not always be the easy way, but there are times that you will have to go through an experience in life, in order to prepare you for your blessings of new beginnings.

> *For the LORD knoweth the way of the righteous: but the way of the ungodly shall perish* ***(Psalm 1:6)****. For our light affliction, which is but for a moment, worketh for us a far more exceeding and eternal weight of glory; While we look not at the things which are seen, but at the things which are not seen: for the things which are seen are temporal; but the things which are not seen are eternal* ***(2 Corinthians 4:17-18)****.*

That's why you give thanks to the Lord in the process of going through, to know that your reward is soon to come. The Kodak moment of your blessing is your shot to share your testimony, so that you may flash and shine on others, to give them hope. The experiences that you suffer through, in your journey, will not compare to the blessings that will unfold for your life.

> *For I reckon that the sufferings of this present time are not worthy to be compared with the glory which shall be revealed in us* ***(Romans 8:18)****.*

Don't become a sellout or a tradeoff, to go a route that's not your ordained purpose, to tail/tell someone else's dreams for their purpose. If you tail/tell someone else's trademark in the place of your life's purpose, then how can you make a true name for yourself, to be a light to shine on someone else? You would, then, be bought for a retail price, and the tradeoff may be through darkness. Therefore, your life will not be tailor-made, but trader-made, so you will not be a teller that speaks for yourself. If you were tailored for another person's destiny, then you would be suited for their lifestyle. Your life is too valuable to be brought down/bought down to a price. Through God, time will be on your side, because you will win every time. If God gives you your own unique purpose for life, then how can you be matched with someone else?

Perhaps, if someone matched with you, in your ordained gift or calling, that you knew you were the best at, will you be heated for a rematch? If you continuously have a rematch with your opponent, going head to head with each other, in adventurous combat, then eventually you would be burned out. It would be better to work together as a team, as two matched heads burning with ideas, to expand and reach others? Now, that beats a heated argument.

It is better to trust in the LORD than to put confidence in man ***(Psalm 118:8)****. Then spake Jesus again unto them, saying, I am the light of the world: he that followeth me shall not walk in darkness, but shall have the light of life* ***(John 8:12)****.*

"Let God Be Your Ruler"

If God is The Ruler of our path, then we should not be re-lured by the path of man, going in many wrong directions. That God is Ruler, then man re-lures.

Re-lur (relure) is ruler spelled backwards.

The definition of lure: to tempt someone to do something.

Wouldn't you rather be led the right way, by The Ruler the first time, than to be re-lured down the wrong path, two or more times?

Thy word is a lamp unto my feet, and a light unto my path ***(Psalm 119:105)****. It is better to trust in the LORD than to put confidence in man* ***(Psalm 118:8)****.* There is a way which seemeth right unto a man, but the end thereof are the ways of death ***(Proverbs 14:12)***.

If you were lead/led by a pencil, to draw you closer to Christ, will your picture come to life? Perhaps, it would be a still life.

Moreover, if you were drawn by a pencil from man's directions, which way are you being led/lead?

Furthermore, if we are supposed to look like Christ, then will your image come to life? If not, then perhaps, you would have the opportunity to erase your mistakes, and start over. But, if you were penned/pinned, would your writes/rights come to life, or will you be setup to be pinned/penned through a conned-track/contract, where you can't wrestle your way out? Perhaps, you can't get up, nor can you erase your errors.

Have you ever drawn yourself to a sign too quickly to stop? It can be impatience for reading the fine print, before signing your name. Maybe, you have a drive to get somewhere in life, but God's signs and wonders will keep you on track. If a train wheel is one inch off the track, it cannot get on rail by itself. If you were a ruler away from God, then how can you stay connected to God if someone else is your ruler, who trains you, by their training wills/wheels, to keep you on their track, if not off track? If man doesn't train in the ways of God, then isn't man's track record going in different directions, other than God's training wills/wheels? We cannot get on track by ourselves, and man (by himself) will re-lure you in the opposite direction. That's why we all need the writes/rights of God to keep us on course.

> *And now, brethren I wot that through ignorance ye did it, as did also your rulers* ***(Acts 3:17)****. All scripture is given by inspiration of God, and is profitable for doctrine, for reproof, for correction, for instruction in righteousness* ***(2 Timothy 3:16)****:*

To be re-lured in a wrong direction, may keep you miles away from your destination. But, if you choose God to be The Ruler of your life, then you may be only a foot to your dreams. Isn't a ruler also a foot?

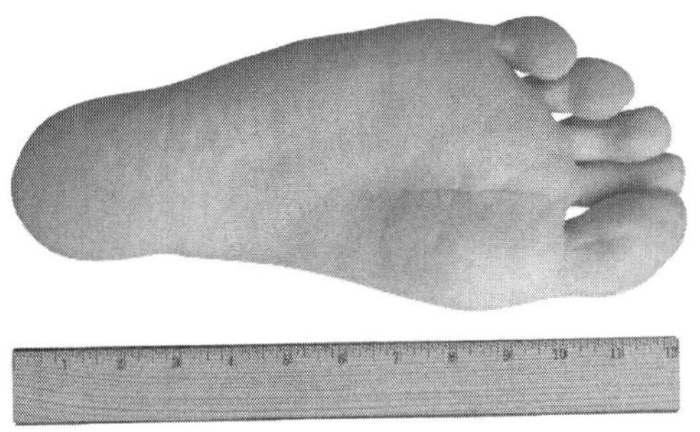

With that being said, God isn't that far from you. As a ruler equals to a foot, then shouldn't your walk be in the ways of God, if He is your Ruler?

> *Lest Satan should get an advantage of us: for we are not ignorant of his devices* ***(2 Corinthians 2:11)****. If we live in the Spirit, let us also walk in the Spirit* ***(Galatians 5:25)****.*

A ruler created by man, is also assumed to be evenly measured to one foot, with all 12 inches measuring exactly the same. But, do you not know that no one in this world is perfect?

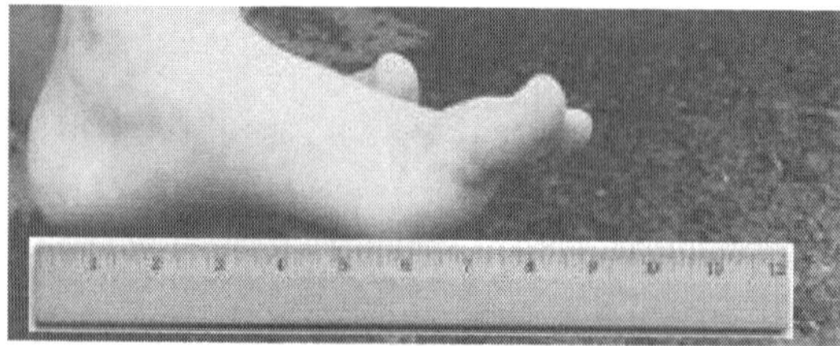

Many of our feet are shorter than a ruler made of man. But, we all come short of the glory of God, who is Ruler over us. We may try to reach perfection, but neither one of us are 100% correct. Therefore, why trust in man's judgment, when God, being our Ruler, goes beyond the measure of man?

> *Who can understand his errors? cleanse thou me from secret faults **(Psalm 19:12)**.*

God also measures time, the weight of water, and He supplies to each one of us, a measure of faith, what a man's ruler has no authority over. If you don't have one foot to walk on, then God is still your Ruler to guide your walk of faith through Him. If your walk in God are feet away, then can't you see your journey ahead? Moreover, if your walk are blocks away from the Lord, then who's blocking your vision? Perhaps, you would need to do a "U-turn/You turn" in the right direction.

> *Where there is no vision, the people perish: but he that keepeth the law, happy is he **(Proverbs 29:18)**. And shall say, Cast ye up, cast ye up, prepare the way, take*

up the stumblingblock out of the way of my people ***(Isaiah 57:14)***.

Have you ever looked at a footage and asked yourself, "Can I be like that someday?" If God has ordained a purpose for each one of us, then what would be the length of your walk, in footage, to reach another person's destiny? That one mile equals to 5,280 feet, and if your legs were worn out, how many steps will it take you to master, or more less, learn someone else's ordained gift, that isn't the call that God had for you?

"CAN YOUR FAITH GO THE EXTRA MILE TO WALK A FOOTAGE ON WATER? MOREOVER, HOW STRONG IS YOUR FAITH WALK ON FOOTAGE, SO OTHERS CAN SEE/SEA LIKE YOU?"

Picture this:

"CAN YOU STAND THE TEST OF YOUR FOOTAGE ON WATER? IF NOT, THEN HOW CAN YOU RUN A FOOTAGE AND STAY ON TOP OF THINGS?"

*A man's heart deviseth his way: but the LORD directeth his steps **(Proverbs 16:9)**.*

If we don't lose our faith, and keep our trust in the Lord, we can stay above the waters. Thus, we will not sink as Peter began to. If we stay focused, through our every walk of life, with faith and confidence in God, then we will not have to take a re-Peter's/repeater's course. The strong winds blew Peter's faith away, so he failed the test during/doing his walk to Jesus.

*But straightway Jesus spake unto them, saying, Be of good cheer; it is I; be not afraid. And Peter answered him and said, Lord, if it be thou, bid me come unto thee on the water. And he said, Come. And when Peter was come down out of the ship, he walked on the water, to go to Jesus. But when he saw the wind boisterous, he was afraid; and beginning to sink, he cried, saying, Lord, save me. And immediately Jesus stretched forth his hand, and caught him, and said unto him, O thou of little faith, wherefore didst thou doubt **(Matthew 14:27-31)**?*

It's amazing how someone may get jealous of another person's talents. In time, they will stretch themselves, to put their foot in their mouth. Perhaps, they would get bent out of shape by a long stretch. But, why talk bad of someone that you wish to be like?

*For who maketh thee to differ from another? and what hast thou that thou didst not receive? now if thou didst receive it, why dost thou glory, as if thou hadst not received it **(1 Corinthians 4:7)**?*

Moreover, if you have thoughts to endorse yourself into someone else's gifts, don't you know that God will bless you with talents beyond your wildest dreams? Many people are blessed with talents to put their foot in a home cooked meal.

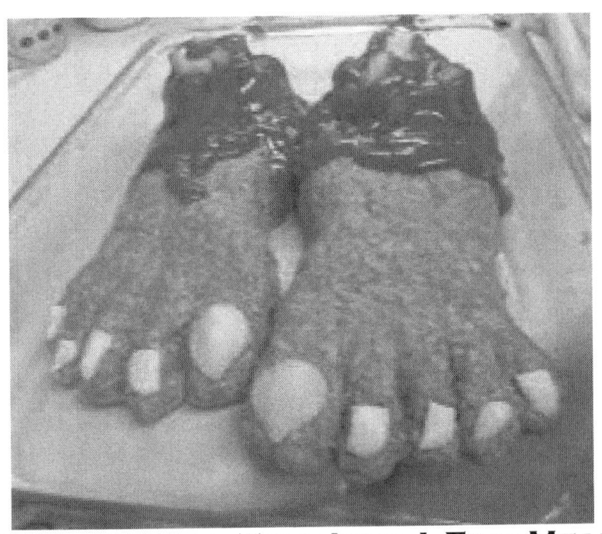

"STICKING YOUR TOES INTO A FINE MEAL"

Your blessings will come in perfect timing. No one can measure time like God. He measures time perfectly, as the Ruler that He is. That God is our Ruler, don't think of Him as a straight line to measure our distance. Think of God, our Ruler, as the answer to the straight narrow path that will keep us in line, as we go the distance, for eternal life, through His word.

> *And we know that all things work together for good to them that love God, to them who are the called according to his purpose* ***(Romans 8:28)***.

"A Hoary Story"

How valuable is your hair? It is said that knowledge is money. Therefore, isn't wisdom also a wealth of riches? If the hairs on your head are silver, then how rich are you in wisdom? Perhaps, the hair flow of silver treasures are flourishing from your gold-mind/goldmine.

Do you bank on the wisdom that God has given you? If so, then have you checked the account of your hairs? Isn't it amazing how God knows the count of each one of our hairs? God also knows our value more than we know ourselves.

> *Commit thy works unto the LORD, and thy thoughts shall be established* ***(Proverbs 16:3)****. But even the very hairs of your head are all numbered. Fear not therefore: ye are of more value than many sparrows* ***(Luke 12:7)****.*

If you, as a generation of silver, cannot keep up with the hair count from your heads, then why ask for millions of dollars that are well over the hairs that you refused to count? Now, if you could keep up with the count of your hairs, then you would have counted rolls of silver. Perhaps, you will be rolling in dough.

> *The hoary head is a crown of glory, if it be found in the way of righteousness* ***(Proverbs 16:31)****. For wisdom is a defence, and money is a defence: but the excellency of knowledge is, that wisdom giveth life to them that have it* ***(Ecclesiastes 7:12)****.*

Furthermore, you will see dollar signs ($).

> *With thy wisdom and with thine understanding thou hast gotten thee riches, and hast gotten gold and silver into thy treasures* ***(Ezekiel 28:4)****:*

If you lost some of your hairs of silver, do you know how many hairs you have left? Furthermore, how much have you lost in rolls? Have you been ripped off? Perhaps, the count of hairs are too much for you to handle! Then, how can you manage the amount in which you are wishing for in millions of dollars?

> *For which of you, intending to build a tower, sitteth not down first, and counteth the cost, whether he have sufficient to finish it? Lest haply, after he hath laid the foundation, and is not able to finish it, all that behold it begin to mock him, Saying, This man began to build, and was not able to finish* ***(Luke 14:28-30)****.*

"Proving That God Is Good Alpha-braically"

Coming from an Alpha-braic/algebraic perspective, to prove that GOD is GOOD:

In this Alpha-matical (mathematical) equation, the word "is" is equivalent to equal (=).

Example: 1 + 1 is 2. In the same manner, 1 + 1 = 2.

Therefore, knowing that GOD is GOOD, in the like manner, we arrive to:

GOD = GOOD.

The letter "O" is the abbreviation for "One". Therefore:

O = One = 1, and, also

Alpha = First = 1st = 1

In this Alpha-matical/mathematical equation, wherever there is an "O", replace it with a "1":

GOD = GOOD

G(1)D = G(1)(1)D

1GD = 1^2GD

As a Math-of-fact (matter of fact), one (1) to any power is still one (1). That's why God is God all by Himself. Perhaps, that's because God is all power in Himself, and He is One! Giving you:

1GD = 1GD

GD = GD

Therefore, GOD is GOOD! Moreover, GOD is GOD! Furthermore, without GOD, there's no GOOD, and without GOOD, where is GOD?

Since God is Alpha and Omega, I will prove that GOD is GOOD from an Omega's perspective:

O1 = Omega, and O2 = One = 1

G(O1)D = G(O1)(O2)D

G(Omega)D = G(Omega)(1)D

GOmegaD = GOmega(1)D
GO mega! GO mega! ♫

DEFINITION OF MEGA – VERY LARGE; HUGE.

Whatever is multiplied by "1", it will equal to itself. Furthermore, I will combine all like letters together, giving me:

GODmega = (1)GODmega

GODmega = GODmega

Isn't GOD GOOD, and isn't GOD also OMEGA? He is GOD of all gods, and the aftermath of the problem reconfirms that He is GOD all by Himself, for the reason that HE is 1. Now, you do the math!

> *Great is our Lord, and of great power: his understanding is infinite* ***(Psalm 147:5)****. And when he was gone forth into the way, there came one running, and kneeled to him, and asked him, Good Master, what shall I do that I may inherit eternal life? And Jesus said unto him, Why callest thou me good? there is none good but one, that is God* ***(Mark 10:17-18)****. I am Alpha and Omega, the beginning and the end, the first and the last* ***(Revelation 22:13)****.*

PART 2: ON-BRAND FOOD FOR THOUGHT QUOTES AND POETRY

"Why Speak 'Might Be Able To'?"

If you take a test, and from 0% to 100%, you score a 50%, you will fail. Furthermore, if you speak the words, "I might be able to pass that test." You just put yourself at a 50% chance of passing. Therefore, why limit yourself to 50%, and why limit yourself by the might (maybe) and might (power) of your thoughts to cause a stronghold on your life? If you take away the maybes by the might of your tongue, you will score higher in life.

> *Death and life are in the power of the tongue: and they that love it shall eat the fruit thereof* ***(Proverbs 18:21)****. I know thy works, that thou art neither cold nor hot: I would thou wert cold or hot. So then because thou art lukewarm, and neither cold nor hot, I will spue thee out of my mouth* ***(Revelations 3:15-16)****. No man can serve two masters: for either he will hate the one, and love the other; or else he will hold to the one, and despise the other. Ye cannot serve God and mammon* ***(Matthew 6:24)****.*

"Why Walk Around With A Chip On Your Shoulder"

Why is it that people walk around with a chip on their shoulder when the mouth is where it goes? Have their belly run out of space, so they found another storage place? Maybe they didn't want to share and just walk around with a spare. It can be a chip that people want to chew at as they get older, so they'd rather keep that spare weight over their shoulder. Many times, we put pressure on ourselves, and that many chips on one shoulder is not good for our health. As we put on our shoulders that much weight, before we know it, we'll be bent out of shape, and sooner or later, we'll break. As it is said that communication is the key, there are times that you have to share your chips with a group, teammate, or family, so pass some of your chips over. In that way, they won't all rest on your shoulder. Aren't many of us putting more on our plates than we can handle? Moreover, are we putting on more than what the plate can handle? If we are stressing from a chip on our shoulder, how long can one stand for a bag of chips? On the contrary, that a bag of chips can put a person into misery before one chip, then I wonder, what are they putting into our food?" Therefore, we should watch what we eat, because what we eat can be the substance of our attitude.

> *BE YE ANGRY, AND SIN NOT: let not the sun go down upon your wrath (**Ephesians 4:26**): Let all bitterness, and wrath, and anger, and clamour, and evil speaking, be put away from you, with all malice: And be ye kind one to another, tenderhearted, forgiving one another, even as God for Christ's sake hath forgiven you (**Ephesians 4:31-32**). Brethren, I count not myself to have apprehended: but this one thing I do, forgetting those things which are behind, and reaching forth unto those things which are before, I press toward the mark for the prize of the high calling of God in Christ Jesus (**Philippians 3:13-14**). Remember ye not the former things, neither consider the things of old. Behold, I will do a new thing; now it shall spring forth; shall ye not know it? I will even make a way in the wilderness, and rivers in the desert (**Isaiah 43:18-19**). But I keep under my body, and bring it into subjection: lest that by any means, when I have preached to others, I myself should be a castaway (**1 Corinthians 9:27**). He that hath no rule over his own spirit is like a city that is broken down, and without walls (**Proverbs 25:28**).*

"Why Do We Complain?"

It has been said, "Today was a long day, and I'm too tired to do anything else." Why do we complain when time seems to go by so slow? But we also dance to a slow tune with happiness and joy. This doesn't mean that a person's dance needs a fine tune-up. We only have one life to live. Enjoy the slow times while you can. On the contrary, we complain when time seems to go by too fast, but we seem to dance to a fast tune with joy.

> *Neither murmur ye, as some of them also murmured, and were destroyed of the destroyer* ***(1 Corinthians 10:10)****. Wherefore, my beloved, as ye have always obeyed, not as in my presence only, but now much more in my absence, work out your own salvation with fear and trembling. For it is God which worketh in you both to will and to do of his good pleasure. Do all things without murmurings and disputings: That ye may be blameless and harmless, the sons of God, without rebuke, in the midst of a crooked and perverse nation, among whom ye shine as lights in the world; Holding forth the word of life; that I may rejoice in the day of Christ, that I have not run in vain, neither laboured in vain* ***(Philippians 2:12-16)****. In every thing give thanks: for this is the will of God in Christ Jesus concerning you* ***(1 Thessalonians 5:18)****.*

"Thinking Through The Holy Spirit Because He Is Our Head"

It's the Holy Spirit who thinks ahead through us, but the Lord also gives us a head to think.

> *But when they shall lead you, and deliver you up, take no thought beforehand what ye shall speak, never do ye premeditate: but whatsoever shall be given you in that hour, that speak ye: for it is not ye that speak, but the Holy Ghost* ***(Mark 13:11)****. Who hath put wisdom in the inward parts? or who hath given understanding to the heart* ***(Job 38:36)****? Let this mind be in you, which was also in Christ Jesus* ***(Philippians 2:5)****.*

"Under The Same Umbrella"

As a couple were walking out of a building, it was raining with the winds blowing hard. The guy's umbrella took a shift in an upward position. As rain was pouring down on him, he needed a shield of protection. Therefore, his wife walking beside him had an extra umbrella where they both shared. God's plan for husband and wife is to operate under the same umbrella, and to never become separated, especially through the storms.

Therefore shall a man leave his father and his mother, and shall cleave unto his wife: and they shall be one flesh ***(Genesis 2:24)****. And the rain descended, and the floods came, and the winds blew, and beat upon that house; and it fell not: for it was founded upon a rock* ***(Matthew 7:25).***

"God Can Turn What Was Meant For Bad To Good"

A Pastor called a young man, by the name of Dexter, up to the altar to pray for both his feet. The Bishop (by the Holy Spirit), told Dexter to sit down, take his shoes off, and for him to touch his own feet. The Bishop said, "Thank God!" Dexter started to thank God for his healing, and his feet were healed. Little did Dexter know, the Bishop was thanking God, because he did not have to touch his feet. Many times, words that people speak are meant for bad, but God can turn them around to mean something good.

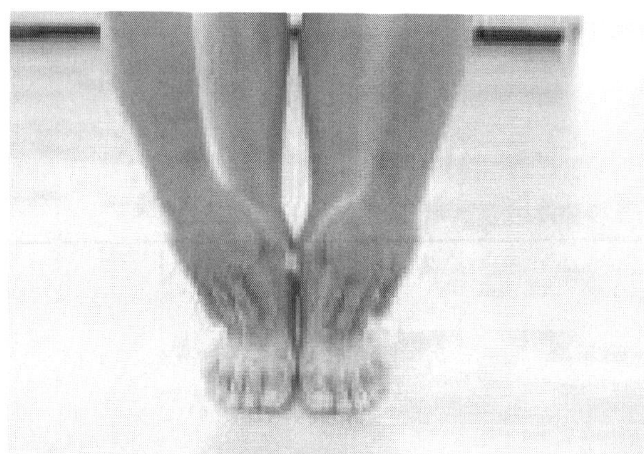

But as for you, ye thought evil against me; but God meant it unto good, to bring to pass, as it is this day, to save much people alive ***(Genesis 50:20)****. And we know that all things work together for good to them that love God, to them who are the called according to His purpose* ***(Romans 8:28)****.*

"God's Word Has More Protection Than A Hood"

Many people seem to show no fear by living in the hood, where a bullet can go through so easily. Why is it that we are so slow to abide in God's word who is our shield of protection from all darts? His word has more coverage than a hood.

> *He shall cover thee with his feathers, and under wings shalt thou trust: his truth shall be thy shield and buckler. Thou shalt not be afraid for the terror by night; nor for the arrow that fileth by day* ***(Psalms 91:4-5)****; Above all, taking the shield of faith, wherewith ye shall be able to quench all the fiery darts of the wicked. And take the helmet of salvation, and the sword of the Spirit, which is the word of God* ***(Ephesians 6:16-17)****.*

"Speak It To Seek It"

You have to speak peace to seek peace. If you don't speak it, then you will decrease it. Therefore, you have to speak the vision to reach the vision. If you don't speak the vision by faith, then you will breach your dreams/desires to waste. If you speak your vision in doubt, then your dreams/desires will U-turn farther out.

> *What man is he that desireth life, and loveth many days, that he may see good? Keep thy tongue from evil, and thy lips from speaking guile. Depart from evil, and do good; seek peace, and pursue it* ***(Psalms 34:12-14)****.*

"Don't Go From A Diamond To Chicken"

I had a talk with a woman by the name of Diamond, who said that she didn't know what her gift was nor her purpose in life. Diamond stated that she was too chicken to do ministry. I replied, "You should never claim yourself to be chicken. That only allows Satan to eat you alive."

Be not deceived; God is not mocked: for whatsoever a man soweth, that shall he also reap ***(Galatians 6:7)****. A man's gift maketh room for him, and bringeth him before great men* ***(Proverbs 18:16)****. For God hath not given us the spirit of fear; but of power, and of love, and of a sound mind* ***(2 Timothy 1:7)****. And there are three that bear witness in earth, the spirit, and the water, and the blood: and these three agree in one* ***(1 John 5:8)****.*

"Don't Look Back"

The things to look forward to, you are blinded by them, because the things of the past, in looking back, you are reminded of them. Moreover, if you are looking back at your past, how can you see in front of you for what's to come?

> *FOR YET A LITTLE WHILE, AND HE THAT SHALL COME WILL COME, AND WILL NOT TARRY. NOW THE JUST SHALL LIVE BY FAITH: BUT IF ANY MAN DRAW BACK, MY SOUL SHALL HAVE NO PLEASURE IN HIM. But we are not of them who draw back unto perdition; but of them that believe to the saving of the soul* ***(Hebrews 10:37-39)****. And Jesus said unto him, No man, having put his hand to the plough, and looking back, is fit for the kingdom of God* ***(Luke 9:62)****.*

"Don't Let Others Value You"

When you take charge of your life, you will value yourself. When you value yourself, you can't hold a price with a charge. If you let others value you, they may only put a charge on you that's not worth your value. Moreover, the charge that others may value your worth is not worth your time. Your value is life, and life does not hold a price.

> *All things are lawful unto me, but all things are not expedient: all things are lawful for me, but I will not be brought under the power of any* ***(1 Corinthians 6:12)****. I will make a man more precious than fine gold; even a man than the golden wedge of O'-phir* ***(Isaiah 13:12)****.*

"Give Satan No Glory"

When you snap at people, Satan uses it as a tune to dance as a snapping of fingers to a melody.

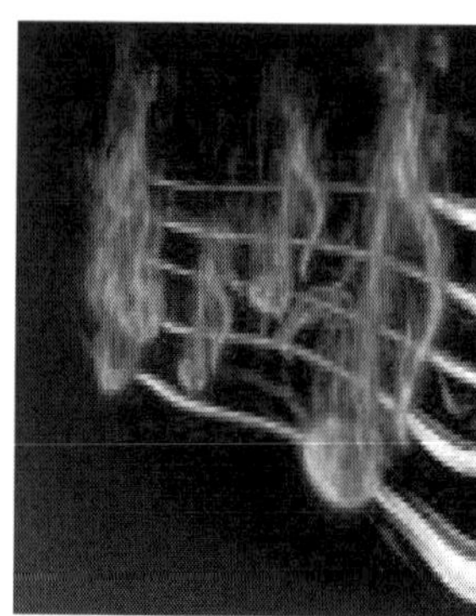

BE YE ANGRY, AND SIN NOT: let not the sun go down on your wrath ***(Ephesians 4:26-27)****: A SOFT answer turnth away wrath: but grievous words stir up anger. The tongue of the wise useth knowledge aright: but the mouth of fools poureth out foolishness* ***(Proverbs 15:1-2)****.*

"Your Body Is A Treasure Of Silver and Gold"

If your eyes are as a watch, and a watch is as a piece of jewelry, then your body should be treasured as a temple of silver and gold.

> *What? know ye not that your body is the temple of the Holy Ghost which is in you, which ye have of God, and ye are not your own* ***(1 Corinthians 6:19)****? Every man according as he purposeth in his heart, so let him give; not grudgingly, or of necessity: for God loveth a cheerful giver* ***(2 Corinthians 9:7)****.*

"Fear The Lord & Not The Adversary"

If the Lord is our comfort, and we are supposed to make a joyful noise for Him, why then do we make a fearful noise for the adversary, to give him joy?

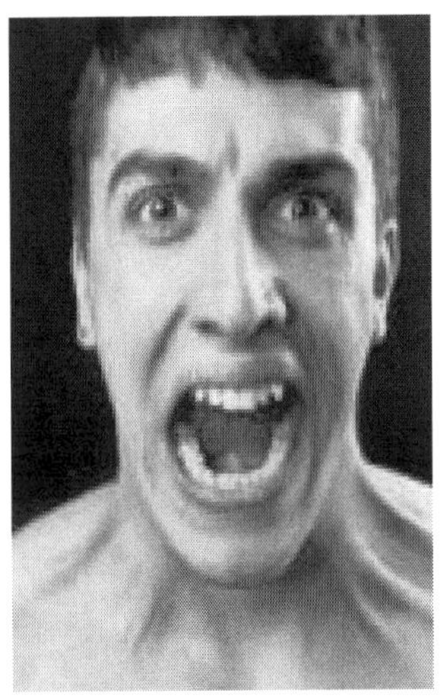

> *Make a joyful noise unto God, all ye lands: Sing forth the honour of His name: make his praise glorious* ***(Psalms 66:1-2)****. He restoreth my soul: He leadeth me in the paths of righteousness for His name's sake. Yea, though I walk through the valley of the shadow of death, I will fear no evil: for thou art with me; thy rod and thy staff they comfort me* ***(Psalms 23:3-4).***

"Why Cry out For Our Earthly Parents But Not Our Heavenly Parent?"

If we, as a baby in a crib, has cried out for our parents, here on Earth, to change our diapers, why is it that we are so uptight, and don't want to cry out to our Father in heaven, when He will reach out to change us after we have made a mess?

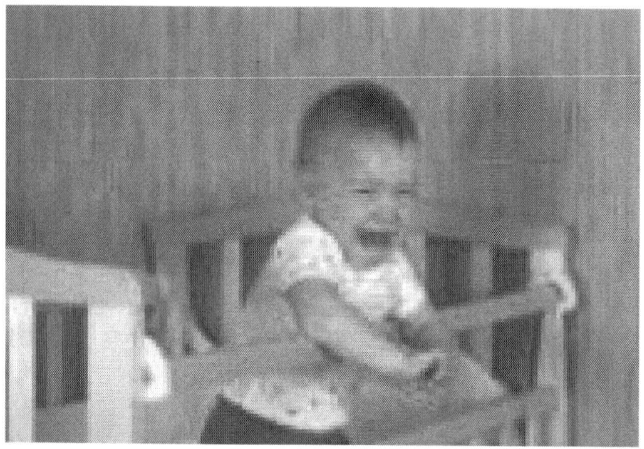

*But let man and beast be covered with sackcloth, and cry mightily unto God: yea, let them turn every one from his evil way, and from the violence that is in their hands **(Jonah 8:3)**. If we confess our sins, He is faithful and just to forgive us our sins, and to cleanse us from all unrighteousness **(1 John 1:9)**.*

"You Be The King Of Your Castle"

The castle is your body. Don't let Satan come in. Don't let Satan be the crook and destroy you with his rook. Moreover, don't let him make you into a rookie when you are already made King/Queen of your castle.

> *What? know ye not that your body is the temple of the Holy Ghost which is in you, which ye have of God, and ye are not your own? For ye are bought with a price: therefore glorify God in your body, and in your spirit, which are God's* ***(1 Corinthians 6:19-20)****. And what agreement hath the temple of God with idols? for ye are the temple of the living God; as God hath said, I will dwell in them, and walk in them; and I will be their God, and they shall be my people* ***(2 Corinthians 6:16)****.*

"Time Is Not Your Friend"

A Pastor once said, "Time is not your friend." When I thought about that, my thoughts expounded on these conclusions:

- Time does not wait on you, but a friend does.
- In time, we all grow as if time is our mentor because, we all grow in time.
- A clock has three hands, but it never stops to give us a hand when we are in need, yet, a friend does.
- Time counts for itself, so we can't count on time (to wait on us).

- Just like a baby, we can't take our eyes off of time; because, you can't depend on time to stay still.

  Example: When you close your eyes and go to sleep, time moves so quickly. We awaken from a sleep and wonder where time has gone.

- As children, we claimed some individuals as our friends when they were against us. Time is also against us. As a child gains knowledge through time, time doesn't last forever, and neither does our knowledge. It starts to fade away with time. On that note, can time be as a thief in the night, or perhaps, any parts of the day? A true friend will not still your moment of joy.

Blessed is he that readeth, and they that hear the words of this prophecy, and keep those things which are written therein: for the time is at hand ***(Revelation 1:3).***

"Don't Suck It Up Give It To God"

When something appears to go wrong, I've heard the expression, "Suck it up!" Why would you suck up what's not good for your system? I'd rather let it go and give it to God.

> *Humble yourselves therefore under the mighty hand of God, that he may exalt you in due time: Casting all your care upon him; for he careth for you* ***(1 Peter 5:6-7)****.*

"Look To God Not Man"

Why is it that we depend on others for a handout, when our Father in Heaven has His hand out for us? Is not His hand bigger than ours, here on Earth? Moreover, isn't the world in the palm of His hands?

> *O my God, I trust in thee: let me not be ashamed, let not mine enemies triumph over me* ***(Psalm 25:2)****. Put not your trust in princes, nor in the son of man, in whom there is no help* ***(Psalm 146:3)****.*

"Giving You A Piece Of My Mind"

When people come to a disagreement, often times they become angry, and many have a dispute. It is often said, "I'm going to give you a piece of my mind." I believe that we need our whole mind that God had given us. If you give someone a piece of your mind, you will lose it. I'd rather tell you what's on my mind. To give someone a piece of your mind, is for keeps. You may go stir crazy until you find a replacement. But I can assure you, that you will not be your true self. Another way to emphasize this statement is, "If you give someone a piece of your mind, you will lose a piece/peace with yourself."

> *And be renewed in the spirit of your mind; And that ye put on the new man, which after God is created in righteousness and true holiness* ***(Ephesians 4:23-24)****. Thou wilt keep him in perfect peace, whose mind is stayed on thee: because he trusteth in thee* ***(Isaiah 26:3)****. Be ye angry, and sin not: let not the sun go down upon your wrath: Neither give place to the devil* ***(Ephesians 4:26-27)****.*

"Just Trust Him"

When it comes to God, you can't rush Him, you can't hush Him, you can't fuss at Him, all you can do is trust Him.

Trust in the LORD with all thine heart; and lean not unto thine own understanding ***(Proverbs 3:5)****. But if we hope for that we see not, then do we with patience wait for it* ***(Romans 8:25)****. Wait on the LORD: be of good courage, and he shall strengthen thine heart: wait, I say, on the LORD* ***(Psalm 27:14)****.*

"Babies Ruling The World"

Kids were playing in a restaurant as they were also trying to keep the baby under control. The baby banged her head under the table and started crying. The adults got up from the table to put the baby's coat on. As the family were walking toward the door to leave the restaurant, the baby said very clearly, "Bye (as she suddenly stopped crying)! Sometimes, it takes the head of a baby to think for adults. *(True Story)*

And I will give children to be their princes, and babes shall rule over them ***(Isaiah 3:4)****.*

"My Way Or The Highway"

It has been said, "It will be my way, or the highway." Me personally, I'd rather take the highway, because my trust is in God, and not man. God is the high way. Moreover, if you put your trust in men, who are considered other gods, man's highway may lead you to a hangover.

THE HIGHWAY LEADS YOU TO HEAVEN

MAN'S WAY WILL LEAD YOU TO HELL

Thus saith the LORD; Cursed be the man that trusteth in man, and maketh flesh his arm, and whose heart departeth from the LORD ***(Jeremiah 17:5)****. It is better to trust in the LORD than to put confidence in man* ***(Psalm 118:8)****.*

"The Lord's Foundation"

The Lord has laid the foundation of the earth. Why not trust in Him to lay His hands on us, as He has already molded us into His image? Aren't we a part of the Lord's foundation?

Mine hand also hath laid the foundation of the earth, and my right hand hath spanned the heavens: when I call unto them, they stand up together ***(Isaiah 48:13)****.* *And God said, Let us make man in our image, after our likeness: and let them have dominion over the fish of the sea, and over the fowl of the air, and over the cattle, and over all the earth, and over every creeping thing that creepeth upon the earth* ***(Genesis 1:26)****.* *For we are labourers together with God: ye are God's husbandry, ye are God's building* ***(1 Corinthians 3:9)****.* *Now he which stablisheth us with you in Christ, and hath anointed us, is God; Who hath also sealed us, and given the earnest of the Spirit in our hearts* ***(2 Corinthians 1:21-22)****.*

"God Is Alpha, Center And Omega"

As 1 (One) is the beginning, and 3 (Three) is the ending, the number 2 (two) is the center.

Therefore, we arrive to:

1 + 3 = 4 divided by the 2 (Two) numbers: 1 and 3. Therefore,

$$\frac{4 \text{ (The summation of } 1+3)}{2 \text{ (Total numbers to = sum)}} = 2 \text{ (sum of total numbers} \div \text{into its sum)}$$

The number 2 is the center of 1 and 3.

We should see God in that same mathematical format. God is our Alpha and Omega.

The word "And" in mathematical terms means Plus (+).

$$\frac{\text{Alpha + Omega}}{2} = \frac{\text{Beginning + End}}{2} = \text{Center}$$

Therefore, God should be the center of our lives.

> *And He said unto me, It is done. I am Alpha and Omega, the beginning and the end. I will give unto him that is athirst of the fountain of the water of life freely* ***(Revelation 21:6)****. Study to shew thyself approved unto God, a workman that needeth not to be ashamed, rightly dividing the word of truth* ***(2 Timothy 2:15)****.*

"'Might For Maybe' vs 'Might For Strength'"

A friend and I were out working on a project. I said that I wanted to get a certain amount of information typed before the day comes to an end. She stated, "We might reach that quota." I replied, "The word 'Might' should not be in our vocabulary as true believers. We should know that we can do all things for those who believe in God." The only time the word "Might" should be used, is when we, as Christians, are referring to strength.

Example of what a Christian shouldn't say:

- We might be able *to do all things*.

Example of what a Christian should say:

- The Lord gives us the might *to do all things*.

There are times that we must turn negatives into positives. We have to add "The Lord" in our equation, to change our whole situation to be positive.

> *I can do all things through Christ which strengtheneth me* ***(Philippians 4:13)****. Finally, my brethren, be strong in the Lord, and in the power of His might* ***(Ephesians 6:10)****.*

"The Power You Have Over Mountains Based On What Black Pepper & Onions Have Over You"

A small speck of black pepper is sprinkled on a plate, in front of you, and it has the power to serve you with a sneeze, before you have the opportunity to chew into it.

Moreover, it will choke you before you knock it down with a punch (beverage). Furthermore, an onion (that is much larger than that tiny speck of black pepper), but is still much smaller than you, has the power to make you cry with a runny nose, when you cut into it.

With that being said: How much more power does God give us over our mountains, if we only have the faith of a mustard seed which is about the size of a tiny speck of black pepper?

If a tiny specks of black pepper has the power to season an onion with flavour, and an onion has the power to season the taste of food to flavour, then how much more power does God give us to season our mountains, by His favour, to make them move? Doesn't God give us the power over our mountains for every season that we go through?

And Jesus said unto them, Because of your unbelief: for verily I say unto you, If ye have faith as a grain of mustard seed, ye shall say unto this mountain, Remove hence to yonder place; and it shall remove; and nothing shall be impossible unto you ***(Matthew 17:20)***.

"Takeoff And Run With God's Word"

A young man came into a restaurant and saw a few thin books about the Word of God laying on the counter. He asked, "Are these anyone's books? I just don't want to look like I'm stealing." I responded, "You are supposed to take God's word and run with it every chance you get."

I will run the way of thy commandments, when thou shalt enlarge my heart. Teach me, O Lord, the way of thy statues; and I shall keep it unto the end. Give me understanding, and I shall keep thy law; yea, I shall observe it with my whole heart ***(Psalms 119:32-34)***. *Wherefore seeing we also are compassed about with so* *great a cloud of witnesses, let us lay aside every weight, and the sin which doth so easily beset us, and let us run with patience the race that is set before us, Looking unto Jesus the author and finisher of our faith; who for the joy that was set before Him endured the cross, despising the shame, and is set down at the right hand of the throne of God* ***(Hebrews 12:1-2)****.*

"The Bible Is Our Shield"

The Bible is a shield of protection for the darts of evil that are thrown against us.

Wherefore take unto you the whole armour of God, that ye may be able to withstand in the evil day, and having

done all, to stand. Stand therefore, having your loins girt about with truth, and having on the breastplate of righteousness; And your feet shod with the preparation of the gospel of peace; Above all, taking the shield of faith, wherewith ye shall be able to quench all the fiery darts of the wicked. And take the helmet of salvation, and the sword of the Spirit, which is the word of God ***(Ephesians 6:16-17)***.

"Be On One Accord"

In a relationship, if you aren't in one ac/cord (accord), then you may be in for an elect/trick (electric) shock that you can't afford.

In a transaction, when you ask for money to be wired, and the wire details does not match your request, are you not in shock?

Giving thanks always for all things unto God and the Father in the name of our Lord Jesus Christ; Submitting yourselves one to another in the fear of God. Wives, submit yourselves unto your own husbands, as unto the Lord. For the husband is the head of the wife, even as Christ is the head of the church: and he is the saviour of the body. Therefore as the church is subject unto

Christ, so let the wives be to their own husbands in every thing. Husbands, love your wives, even as Christ also loved the church, and gave himself for it ***(Ephesians 5:20-25)****; Lest Satan should get an advantage of us: for we are not ignorant of his devices* ***(2 Corinthians 2:11).***

"The Price Is Christ"

Most of us have heard of the game show, "The Price Is Right". But, have you ever considered "The Price Is Christ"? On the flipside, "Christ Is Right".

What? Know ye not that your body is the temple of the Holy Ghost which is in you, which ye have of God, and ye are not your own? For ye are bought with a price: therefore glorify God in your body, and in your spirit, which are God's ***(1 Corinthians 6:19-20)****. But God commendeth his love toward us, in that, while we were yet sinners, Christ died for us* ***(Romans 5:8)****.*

"Be Careful Who Prays For You"

When a person is being prayed over by one person (at that moment) through prophecy, for that one issue, should a person have two different stories being manifested to him/her for the same issue? Are you not hurt enough from the first prophecy, so you find the need to go to someone else for a second man-ife-story? The only time that more than one person should pray for you, is if they were coming together/to gather into agreement. In some books, isn't there two or three authors that come together in one story? But, if you get knocked down by the spirit, from two different stories, will you not be confused? Moreover, if you were in a two-story apartment building, and you fell from the first story, you may feel some hurt. If you fell from the second story, will you not be injured? If you don't have trust in a man of God to pray for you, why go to two?

> *And all things, whatsoever ye shall ask in prayer, believing, ye shall receive* ***(Matthew 21:22)****. Verily I say unto you, Whatsoever ye shall bind on earth shall be bound in heaven: and whatsoever ye shall loose on earth shall be loosed in heaven. Again I say unto you, That if two of you shall agree on earth as touching any thing that they shall ask, it shall be done for them of my Father which is in heaven. For where two or three are gathered together in my name, there am I in the midst of them* ***(Matthew 18:18-20)****. So then faith cometh by hearing, and hearing by the word of God* ***(Romans***

10:17)*. Now faith is the substance of things hoped for, the evidence of things not seen* ***(Hebrews 11:1)****. But without faith it is impossible to please him: for he that cometh to God must believe that he is, and that he is a rewarder of them that diligently seek him* ***(Hebrews 11:6)****.*

"Why Bounce Back Instead Of Spring Forward"

We are told to bounce back, but if we do so, we attend to the past. Therefore, we should spring forward.

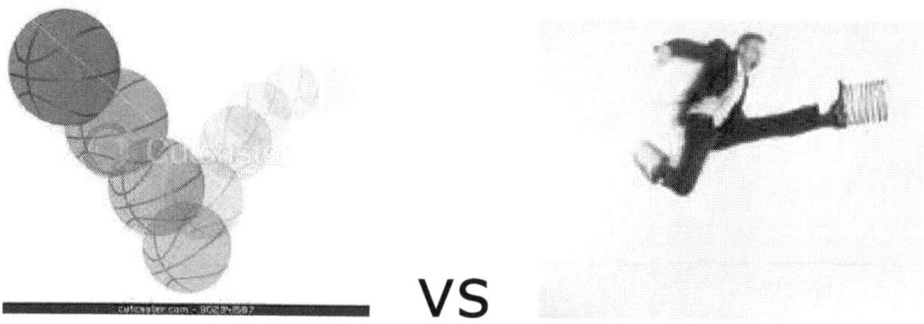

MoReoveR, If we boUnce bACK, SAtAn cAn HAve A bAll on US. But, If we SPRInG foRWARD, we cAn RISe to new HeIGHts.

Remember ye not the former things, neither consider the things of old ***(Isaiah 43:18-19)****. Therefore if any man be in Christ, he is a new creature: old things are passed away; behold, all things are become new* ***(2 Corinthians 5:17)****.*

"Turning From RAW To WAR"

When we are born again as children of God, we will come out of the water RAW, just like rinsing food (in water) before heating it. But, as we become stronger in Christ, He will turn us around for WAR. After being rinsed in baptism, shouldn't we be heated for the Lord, as we become stronger in Christ?

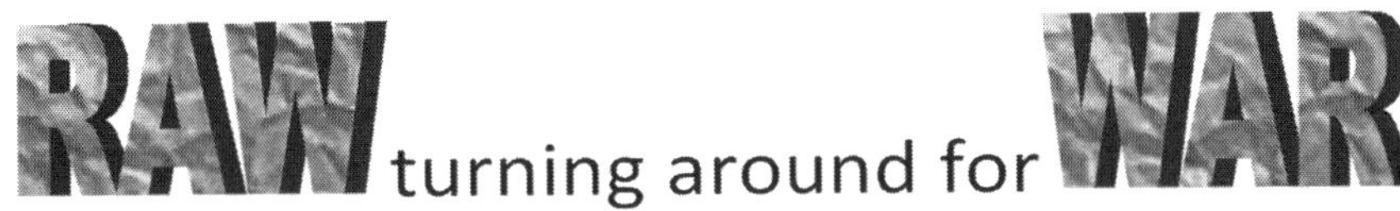

Then Peter said unto them, Repent, and be baptized every one of you in the name of Jesus Christ for the remission of sins, and ye shall receive the gift of the Holy Ghost ***(Acts 2:38)****. Being born again, not of corruptible seed, but of incorruptible, by the word of God, which liveth and abideth for ever* ***(1 Peter 1:23)****. The like figure whereunto even baptism doth also now save us (not the putting away of the filth of the flesh, but the answer of a good conscience toward God,) by the resurrection of Jesus Christ* ***(1 Peter 3:21)****: God is my strength and power: and he maketh my way perfect. He maketh my feet like hinds' feet: and setteth me upon my high places. He teacheth my hands to war; so that a bow of steel is broken by mine arms. Thou hast also given me the shield of thy salvation: and thy gentleness hath made me great. Thou hast enlarged my steps under me; so that my feet did not slip. I have pursued mine enemies, and destroyed them; and turned not again until I had consumed them. And I have consumed them, and wounded them, that they could not arise: yea, they are*

> *fallen under my feet. For thou hast girded me with strength to battle: them that rose up against me hast thou subdued under me* ***(2 Samuel 22:33-40)****. Blessed be the LORD my strength, which teacheth my hands to war, and my fingers to fight: My goodness, and my fortress; my high tower, and my deliverer; my shield, and he in whom I trust; who subdueth my people under me* ***(Psalms 144:1-2)****.*

"Don't Lay Away On God"

When God put your blessings on layaway, trust in Him by continuing to pray away/a way.

> *Pray without ceasing. In every thing give thanks: for this is the will of God in Christ Jesus concerning you* ***(1 Thessalonians 5:17-18)****. Trust in the LORD with all thine heart; and lean not unto thine own understanding. In all thy ways acknowledge him, and he shall direct thy paths* ***(Proverbs 3:5-6)****.*

"Work On Yourself"

Stop trying to compete to be someone else's part, and work on yourself, so that you can be complete in your own heart.

> *And whatsoever ye do in word or deed, do all in the name of the Lord Jesus, giving thanks to God and the Father by him* ***(Colossians 3:17)****. For in him dwelleth all the fulness of the Godhead bodily. And ye are complete in him, which is the head of all principality and power* ***(Colossians 2:9-10)****:*

CHAPTER 2

"ON-BRAND PLAY ON WORDS STORIES/QUOTES AND POETRY"

PART 1

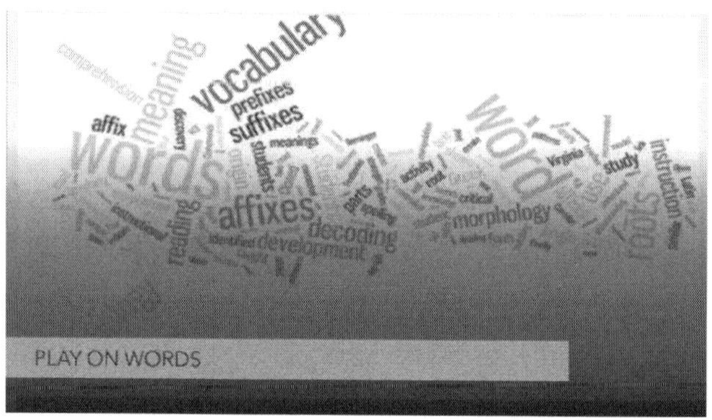

ON-BRAND PLAY ON WORDS STORIES AND POETRY

"In God's Presence/Presents"

To be in God's presence/presents is the best presence/presents that you can have. If you are in God's presence/presents, then you will be amazed with His gifts. For the present time that we live in, is a gift for every moment that we're alive.

> *Thou wilt shew me the path of life: in thy presence is fullness of joy; at thy right hand there are pleasures for evermore* ***(Psalm 16:11)****.*

Is not a gift a present? If you rejoice more in God's presence/presents, then He will bless you with more gifts. If you aren't open in God's presence/presents, then your gifts won't unfold. The Lord loves to rap in His word, as a gift to us, for strength, wisdom, and protection. Therefore, shouldn't we be in the unwrapping business of God's word to share His presence/presents, as a gift, with others, so they can be just, like Him/just like Him?

> *For the wages of sin is death; but the gift of God is eternal life through Jesus Christ our Lord* ***(Romans 6:23)****.*

That God's word is a gift to us, if we meditate in His presence/presents, for an hour of time each day, the Lord will capitalize on hour/our wisdom, for hour/our knowledge, day by day. If knowledge is power, then wouldn't the word of God make you a prophet/profit in the presence/presents of time? The presence of time is [also] the present of time. They both entail "existence" and they both intertwine as a gift to us.

> *Serve the LORD with gladness: come before his presence with singing* ***(Psalm 100:2)****.*

If we are a prophet/profit for God, then how much more will we receive in His riches, than if we were to prophet/profit for ourselves? If you don't receive in God's presence/presents, then would you appreciate His gifts? Moreover, if you don't give a gift, will you be presented a present?

> *Give, and it shall be given unto you; good measure, pressed down, shaken together, and running over, shall men give into your bosom. For with the same measure that ye mete withal it shall be measured to you again* ***(Luke 6:38)****.*

"Can You Tell Time?"

A friend came over to help me with a book project one afternoon. It was starting to get late, while we were both sitting at the kitchen table, working on the project.

She asked: Can I sit where you're sitting?

I responded: Why do you want to sit where I'm sitting? I don't think the chair can take but one person. If you can sit in the same seat where I'm sitting, without the chair falling apart, then I will get the feel of walking in your shoes.

She responded: Okay smarty, I want to exchange seats.

I stated: Ahhhhhhh (As if I didn't already know)! But, why do you want to exchange seats?

She: So I can keep an eye on the time.

Me: Uh, you don't trust me with the time?

She: No! You're good with numbers, and you're good with math, but you can't tell time.

Me: Ain't that about a trip! I can't tell time! You know what? I know that I can't tell time, because when I tell time to stop, it never listens, it keeps running. Time has three hands, but it has no ears. By the way, can you tell a baby? Isn't that something, you can't tell a baby, and then complain that I can't tell time? You know, a baby has ears, and time doesn't. Furthermore, time is God's baby, so why should I tell who God already has total control over? Time is behind God's blueprint. Therefore, can you tell what God is doing behind the skies or His disguise, which is His blueprint? Perhaps, your thoughts will become clouded. Besides God, only time would tell. Time is always good, because it is seasoned to God's taste. There's no wonder why each day is prepared just right.

Ye hypocrites, ye can discern the face of the sky and of the earth; but how is it that ye do not discern this time ***(Luke 12:56)****? It is not for you to know the times or the seasons, which the Father hath put in his own power* ***(Acts 1:7)****.*

Time and a baby, they act just alike. You know why? Because, a baby was born in time. Therefore, both time and baby intertwine.

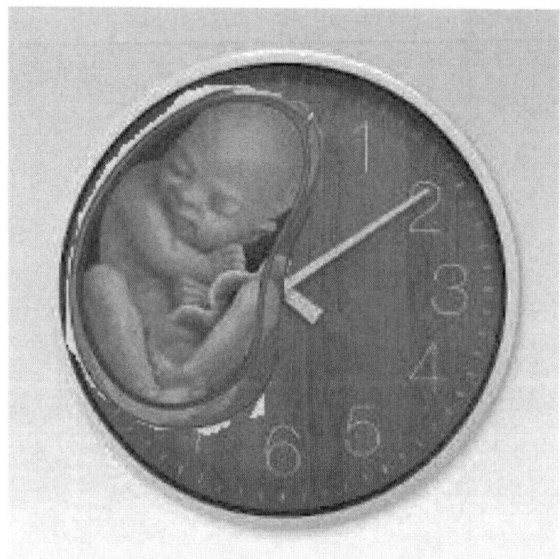

"A Baby Is Born In The Womb Of Time"

That's why they act so much alike. Time has no legs, and they have no feet. That's why it runs with its hands. On the other hand, or shall I say, "...the second hand," a baby isn't so good with their legs or feet, because they were born in time, perhaps, by the second. But, they're so quick with their hands, just like time. Isn't that why a baby gets so ticked and alarmed in a second? Hint: Every second a clock also goes "Tick tock". But, can you blame it when time never sleeps?

Time has three hands, and they do have one eye. Isn't that why it's called a watch? Can you tell time what to do or say in a sign language? Can you tell a baby what to do or say in a sign language, that was just born in time? Perhaps, their eyes are still closed, so what can they watch? Time is like a baby. You have to value it every moment you get. Furthermore, that peace comes in time, how many people have control over peace? If not too many, then who has the power to tell time? That time has millenniums of years ahead of you, and by a watch, time has seen it all, then what knowledge or wisdom can you tell time that has already run circles around you?

He hath made every thing beautiful in his time: also he hath set the world in their heart, so that no man can find out the work that God maketh from the beginning to the end ***(Ecclesiastes 3:11)****. But of that day and that hour knoweth no man, no, not the angels which are in heaven, neither the Son, but the Father. Take ye heed, watch and pray: for ye know not when the time is* ***(Mark 13:32-33)****.*

We all have a time window in life because we were all born into a window of time. A window of time will hold up through a storm, in a breeze. But we, on the other hand, will breakdown in a breeze, and that's in a small window of our time, without the pressure of the storm, in a crisis. With that being said, what does your life reflect on? We can all learn through a timeframe of life, even by an hourglass.

"A TIME WINDOW"

Therefore, because you were born in the presence of your mother's womb, and your mother was born in time, before you, then do you have the right to tell your mother? In respect to that, what gives you the power to tell time, that was created way before your mother? Furthermore, that your mother does not allow you to tell her, as she was born in a "Grand Old Time" of life, before you, then what makes you think that you can tell time, who is a Great Granny to you?

That time passes in a day, and as time also burns by the sun, a day vanishes at no return. Can you reinvent the wheel/will of the sun, day by day? Perhaps, you will be burned out because the sun is fireball of light that is too bright for us to outshine, but we still try to act as if we show time/showtime in the act. Now, can you roll/role like that?

> *All things are full of labour; man cannot utter it: the eye is not satisfied with seeing, nor the ear filled with hearing. The thing that hath been, it is that which shall be; and that which is done is that which shall be done: and there is no new thing under the sun* ***(Ecclesiastes 1:8-9)****.*

I tell you what, you go out and gather thousands of people with picket signs, in the act, for a march against the speed of time, protesting from state to state. In a month, let me know how your protest turned out. Better yet, by faith and prayer, gather 1 or 2 more Prayer Warriors to come in agreement with you, to tell time to stop moving so quickly. But, be careful what you pray for because you may just get what you didn't realize you asked for.

> *And he gave them their request; but sent leanness into their soul* ***(Psalm 106:15)****.*

Your time clock may stop, while other lives keep on living. Moreover, if you made a mistake in the time of day, can you tell time to move backwards? Can you rush time when it is having its moment of peace? It's amazing how we try to blow time, but does time actually speed up or slow down?

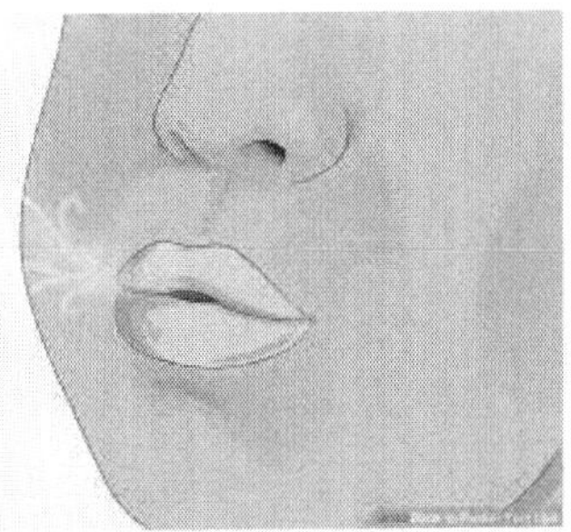

"BLOWING TIME THROUGH A RUSH HOUR"

If it is not so, then who has control over telling time how to operate, but God? In conclusion, that time is God's baby, then why should anyone have business telling a creation that only functions under God's control, who is the creator?

> *Then spake Joshua to the LORD in the day when the LORD delivered up the Am'-or-ites before the children of Israel, and he said in the sight of Israel, Sun, stand thou still upon Gib'-e-on; and thou, Moon, in the valley of Aj'-a-lon. And the sun stood still, and the moon stayed, until the people had avenged themselves upon their enemies. Is not this written in the book of Ja'-sher? So the sun stood still in the midst of heaven, and hasted not to go down about a whole day* ***(Joshua 10:12-13)****.*

"Time" is to enjoy, as we grow in life, but "Time" is not for us to teach a lesson, because we learn lessons through "Time". Therefore, besides God, only "Time" would tell.

> *For whatsoever things were written aforetime were written for our learning, that we through patience and comfort of the scriptures might have hope* ***(Romans 15:4)****.*

On that note, after all was said, you can convey that I got into her tell/tail, and whipped it up into another tell/tale. Oh well, that's the tell/tale/tail end of that one. But, I would like to also state, that as a three-piece suit, this story is suited as a tale-teller/tale, tailor made.

"Unwholesome VS The Whole Sum"

If the words that you speak are unwholesome, then they will come back broken apart in sums of pieces, and they will not return whole. Perhaps, the whole sum of words that you speak can make you or break you.

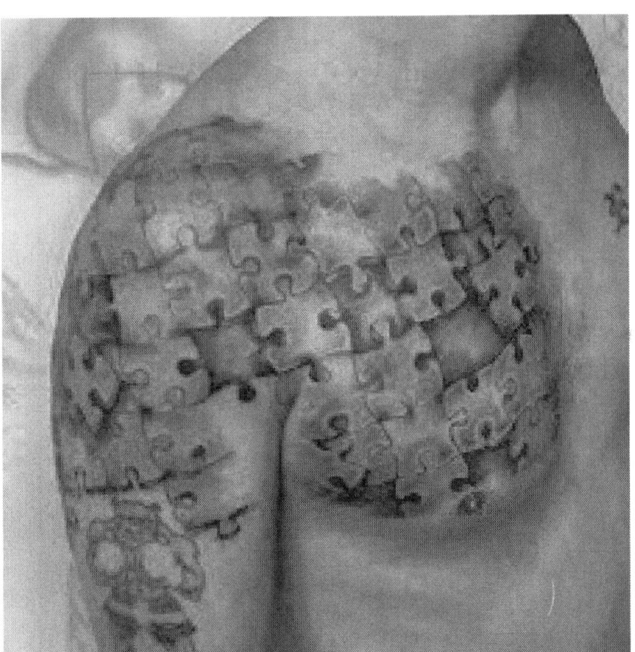

IF YOU ARE BROKEN FOR BEING PUZZLED BY THE WORDS THAT YOU SPEAK, THEN PERHAPS, YOU'VE LOST CONNECTION WITH YOURSELF TO PIECE YOURSELF TOGETHER, FOR A PEACE OF MIND. ON THAT NOTE, ARE YOU LOST FOR WORDS?

Let no corrupt communication proceed out of your mouth, but that which is good to the use of edifying,

> *that it may minister grace unto the hearers* ***(Ephesians 4:29)****. Death and life are in the power of the tongue: and they that love it shall eat the fruit thereof* ***(Proverbs 18:21)****.*

If a puzzle is being put together, and some of the pieces are not in the image, then how can you see the clear vision of the whole picture? If the whole truth is not revealed, then what part of the puzzle is missing?

IF THE HEART OF THE PUZZLE IS MISSING, THEN IS THE SOUL OF THE IMAGE STOLEN?

> *From whom the whole body fitly joined together and compacted by that which every joint supplieth, according to the effectual working in the measure of every part, maketh increase of the body unto the edifying of itself in love* ***(Ephesians 4:16)****.*

If you had a prison term, for not telling the whole story, and your prison time was putting the puzzle together, on how you got there, how long will it take you to figure out the solution to your problem that's 5,000 pieces to the puzzle?

Therefore, tell the whole truth, in the summation of a single image, versus 5,000 pieces, where sums/some of the pieces to the story may easily be lost. Perhaps, you would feel better, in having something to cheese about, because the image will not come back void. It will be a single craft image. That's connecting all of the pieces together in one visual, as it aligns with truth.

> *For as the body is one, and hath many members, and all the members of that one body, being many, are one body: so also is Christ. For by one Spirit are we all baptized into one body, whether we be Jews or Gentiles, whether we be bond or free; and have been all made to drink into one Spirit. For the body is not one member, but many. If the foot shall say, because I am not the hand, I am not of the body; is it therefore not of the*

body? And if the ear shall say, Because I am not the eye, I am not of the body; is it therefore not of the body? If the whole body were an eye, where were the hearing? If the whole were hearing, where were the smelling? But now hath God set the members every one of them in the body, as it hath pleased him. And if they were all one member, where were the body? But now are they many members, yet but one body. And the eye cannot say unto the hand, I have no need of thee: nor again the head to the feet, I have no need of you. Nay, much more those members of the body, which seem to be more feeble, are necessary: And those members of the body, which we think to be less honourable, upon these we bestow more abundant honour; and our uncomely parts have more abundant comeliness. For our comely parts have no need: but God hath tempered the body together, having given more abundant honour to that part which lacked: That there should be no schism in the body; but that the members should have the same care one to another. And whether one member suffer, all the members suffer with it; or one member be honoured, all the members rejoice with it. Now ye are the body of Christ, and members in particular ***(1 Corinthians 12:12-27)****.*

It's amazing how a letter can be left out of a word and change the whole meaning of that word.

Example: A storyline can be told to 10 people (one person at a time). By the time the storyline gets around to the 10th person, the storyline have been changed to something different. Therefore, the storyline was turned into a story-lie. The individual that gave the message last, left the letter "n" out of line. Perhaps, the "n"/end of the storyline was left out from man's true word that was spoken. Because the 10th person did not follow suit, the "n"/end of his word was out of line.

FROM A STORYLINE TO A STORYLIE

But there were false prophets also among the people, even as there shall be false teachers among you, who privily shall bring in damnable heresies, even denying the Lord that bought them, and bring upon themselves swift destruction. And many shall follow their pernicious ways; by reason of whom the way of truth shall be evil spoken of ***(2 Peter 2:1-2)****.*

On the other hand, a word can be left out of a letter, and it will change the whole meaning of that letter.

Example: You have the qualifications for a particular career, and your resume is on point. But, your cover letter is missing one key word that will cause you to lose the opportunity.

As also in all his epistles, speaking in them of these things; in which are some things hard to be understood, which they that are unlearned and unstable wrest, as they do also the other scriptures, unto their own destruction. Ye therefore, beloved, seeing ye know these things before, beware lest ye also, being led away with the error of the wicked, fall from your own stedfastness. But grow in grace, and in the knowledge of our Lord and Saviour Jesus Christ. To him be glory both now and for ever. Amen' ***(2 Peter 3:16-18)****.*

That we all have a timeline for life, will your time lie on Satan's hands, or will you stay in line for God? If your time lies on Satan's hands, as he has lied on you before, he will re-lie/rely on you again, only to destroy your life. It's amazing how a word can change your life. But, on that note, even a letter. Satan comes to steal the letter "f" out of your life, to make it a lie. Moreover, if I let Satan come to steal the "I" out of my LIFE, and LIFE is all capital, then I will not exist. But, if you put your trust in the Lord, your Lifeline will be recovered. Moreover, do you trust in a lifeline, that's created by man, to save your life,

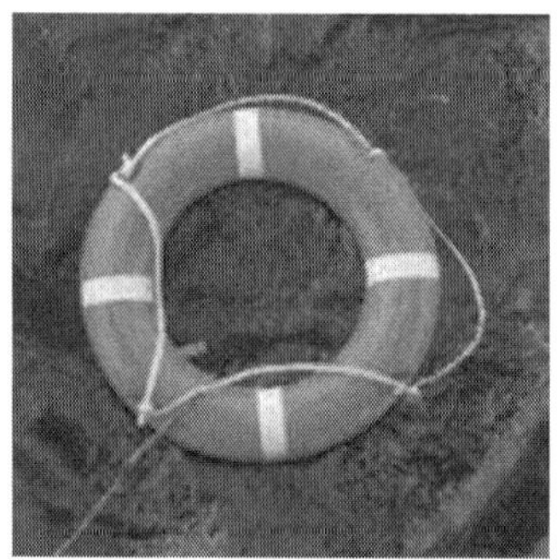

"LIFELINE"

or do you put your trust in the LIFELINE of our savior, Jesus Christ?

> *My times are in thy hand: deliver me from the hand of mine enemies, and from them that persecute me* ***(Psalm 31:15)****. Be sober, be vigilant; because your adversary the devil, as a roaring lion, walketh about, seeking whom he may devour* ***(1 Peter 5:8)****: The thief cometh not, but for to steal, and to kill, and to destroy: I am come that they might have life, and that they might have it more abundantly* ***(John 10:10)****. It is better to trust in the Lord than to put confidence in man* ***(Psalm 118:8)****.*

"Do You Bet Against Alpha?"

It's funny how many people try to tell the word, instead of speaking what the word tells us. On the other hand, aren't many people trying to tell the word what to say, in lieu of listening to what the word is revealing to us? Why do we, in many instances, try to turn a verse around to mean something else?

> *For false Christs and false prophets shall rise, and shall shew signs and wonders, to seduce, if it were possible, even the elect* ***(Mark 13:22)****.*

If "u" were turned around, will not "u" come to an "n"? There are times that we put negative words into our own mouths. If you do that to yourself, would "you" come to "not" for good, or "not" for bad? God created you for a good purpose, so why turn yourself to not, from the way God created you?

you turned around is **noʎ**

> *Surely your turning of things upside down shall be esteemed as the potter's clay: for shall the work say of him that made it, He made it not? or shall the thing framed say of him that framed it, He had no understanding* ***(Isaiah 29:16)****?*

Remember the cereal with alphabets? If words are powerful to the point in which they can cause damage or destruction, then are there not serial/cereal killers?

> *How is the faithful city become an harlot! it was full of judgment; righteousness lodged in it; but now murderers **(Isaiah 1:21)**. Thy tongue deviseth mischiefs; like a sharp rasor, working deceitfully **(Psalm 52:2)**.*

If we are what we eat, then how are the letters that we swallow being formed in our system? Do the letters that we swallow have us cursed? Perhaps, we are puzzled by the words that we digest, that will make us unjust.

"A BIT OF WORD PLAY"

Furthermore, if every word that proceeds out of our mouths are formed with alphabets, and God is Alpha over all of us, then why are letters formed to bet against Alpha?

Alpha-bet

Moreover, in speaking about the cereal, "Alpha-Bits", that we eat our own words, do you trust in a "Bitcoin" over Alpha's Word?

If God doesn't lead us in the teachings of His word, will we not speak vice-versa instead of speaking by God's advice, through His every verse, that is written? Whose advice are we following, or whose vice are we adding? If we follow Christ, we won't fall low of Him.

> *For I testify unto every man that heareth the words of the prophecy of this book, If any man shall add unto these things, God shall add unto him the plagues that are written in this book: And if any man shall take away from the words of the book of this prophecy, God shall take away his part out of the book of life, and out of the holy city, and from the things which are written in this book* ***(Revelation 22:18-19)***.

If we bank on alphabets over God's word, then whom do we put our trust? Moreover, if we don't bank on God's word, and His word is life, then what will we profit from a trust that doesn't exist? Alphabets may spell positive words, but they also spell "Doubt" which is a negative. On that note, if God's word is all truth, then why bet against Alpha?

Every word of God is pure: he is a shield unto them that put their trust in him. Add thou not unto his words, lest he reprove thee, and thou be found a liar ***(Proverbs 30:5-6)***.

"See vs Look"

How close are the words "see" and "look" in meaning? If you are seeing something, aren't you also looking at it? Furthermore, If the word "see" is looking in the mirror, isn't it looking at itself at "ees" (ease)?

SEE | ƎƎƧ

Now, if you see the word "look" in the mirror, wouldn't you see "kool" (cool)?

LOOK | ꓘOOᒧ

Well, aren't you kool (cool) if you are at ees (ease) with yourself?

> *But the LORD said unto Samuel, Look not on his countenance, or on the height of his stature; because I have refused him: for the LORD seeth not as man seeth; for man looketh on the outward appearance, but the LORD looketh on the heart* ***(1 Samuel 16:7)****.*

Let's paraphrase this aspect from another perspective. If a woman designs her eyes to look beautiful, in a bad neighborhood, does that really mean that she can see beauty going down that same path of life? In addition, just because a person cannot see the part in a movie, does not mean that he or she can't look the part in the movie. If a person lost his or her vision, means that they can't see. Therefore, they can't look. But, if someone looks for light, doesn't mean that a person sees for light. To look for light is to search for light, but to see for light, is where the light is the evidence of how we see.

> *While we look not at the things which are seen, but at the things which are not seen: for the things which are seen are temporal; but the things which are not seen are eternal* ***(2 Corinthians 4:18)****. And there shall be no more curse: but the throne of God and of the Lamb shall be in it; and his servants shall serve him: And they shall see his face; and his name shall be in their foreheads. And there shall be no night there; and they need no candle, neither light of the sun; for the Lord God giveth them light: and they shall reign for ever and ever* ***(Revelation 22:3-5)****.*

Now, if you are seeing the purpose for your life, doesn't mean that you are looking the purpose for your life. If you are seeing the purpose for your life, through Christ, then perhaps, you are at "ees" (ease) with your ordained purpose, if you are working in it. On the other hand, if you are looking the purpose for your life, it doesn't mean that you are "Kool" (cool) with it, if you haven't matured and fully developed in your calling. You are just acting the part and not being just, until reality hits you, to make you stronger to appreciate your ordained gift and purpose. Perhaps, you may be trying to hide from it. You may still be unsure about a purpose that you are working in, that could or could not be your ordained one. Therefore, you may or may not even be warm yet. You may still be in the cold. It's hilarious, that if you are Lukewarm, then wouldn't you be by your Mark? Read your Bible!

In addition, just because he or she can't see beautiful, does not mean that he or she can't look beautiful.

Moreover, just because a person without vision cannot see with ees (ease), does not mean that he or she cannot look kool (cool).

He hath made every thing beautiful in his time: also he hath set the world in their heart, so that no man can find out the work that God maketh from the beginning to the end ***(Ecclesiastes 3:11)****. What man is he that feareth the LORD? him shall he teach in the way that he shall choose. His soul shall dwell at ease; and his seed shall inherit the earth* ***(Psalms 25:12-13)****.*

"A Water's Reflection vs A Mirror's Reflection"

The Lord has given us all LIFE, and for all, He has forgiven. When you are baptized under water, aren't you being cleansed, and isn't your LIFE being turned around for rite through Christ?

It is said that facts will reflect truth. That water is pure, doesn't it reveal truth from its clear reflection? Moreover, isn't "LIFE" also turned around for rite, through the image of water?

He that believeth on me, as the scripture hath said, out of his belly shall flow rivers of living water ***(John 7:38)****. And he shewed me a pure river of water of life, clear as crystal, proceeding out of the throne of God and of the Lamb* ***(Revelation 22:1)****. And this is the record, that God hath given us eternal life, and this life is in his Son* ***(1 John 5:11)****.*

God made LigH+. How is LigH+ defined from a water's perspective?

It is obvious that "LIGHT" is also "RIGHT". Furthermore, Jesus is the Light. Didn't God create His Son, who is "Light" of the world? Aren't you blessed that Jesus came across/a cross (+), in your path, to save your life? Isn't that a plus (+)?

> *And God said, Let there be light: and there was light. And God saw the light, that it was good: and God divided the light from the darkness* ***(Genesis 1:3-4)****.* *Then spake Jesus again unto them, saying, I am the light of the world: he that followeth me shall not walk in darkness, but shall have the light of life* ***(John 8:12)****.*

It's amazing how a right angle (in mathematics) can face in either direction, and still be right:

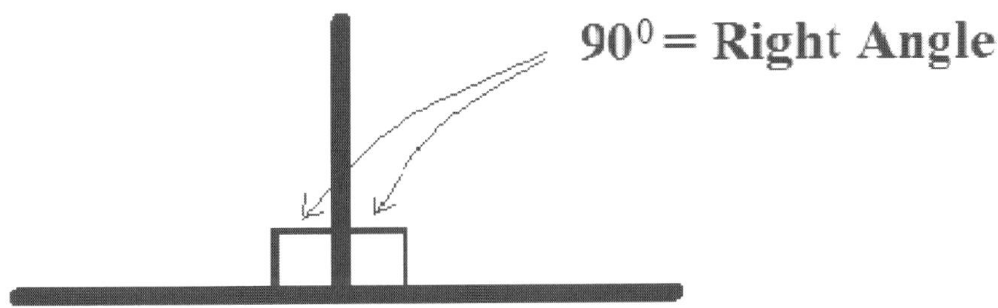

But, when the right angles are collaborated with itself, under water, doesn't it reveal a cross?

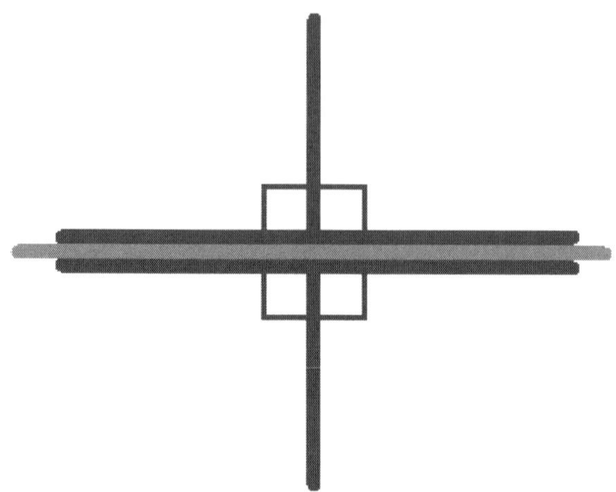

Study to shew thyself approved unto God, a workman that needeth not to be ashamed, rightly dividing the word of truth ***(2 Timothy 2:15)****.*

Perhaps, that's why all angles are right, so that no one gets left behind. Moreover, didn't Jesus give us His all? Since that is the case, as every court has one, then what judgment is wrong about it?

For ways in which people are treated wrong feels unacceptable. But, the things that are correct, through Christ, are made collectables. In the sight of water, isn't "COLLEC+" also "COrrEC+"?

Since everything that is made by God is right, aren't we supposed to receive what He gives us, as a collectable, and then share with others? Moreover, when you feel that you have done everything correct, for a wrong doing, would you want to be judged by a correctional officer, by being given a space for life, in prison, and collect your thoughts, or would you rather be in the prison of the Lord, who offers you space for correction?

> *My son, despise not the chastening of the LORD; neither be weary of his correction: For whom the LORD loveth he correcteth; even as a father the son in whom he delighteth* ***(Proverbs 3:11-12)****.*

We should always put God first and foremost. As a roman numeral, God is "I" (Roman Numeral One).

Coming from a water's perspective, does God change His appearance?

But thou art the same, and thy years shall have no end ***(Psalm 102:27)****.*

Aren't we supposed to be in the image of God? When we characterize ourselves as a first person singular, we are also in the image of "I" (The Letter). Don't we appear as the image of God, who is "I" (Roman Numeral One)? But, our actions are different.

Now, if you take "I" (the letter), and multiply it 3 times, the summation will arrive to:

$$I \times I \times I = I^3 \text{ (I to the 3}^{\text{rd}} \text{ power)}$$

Therefore, a group of 1000 "I's" (people coming together) is:

$$I^{1000} \text{ (I to the one thousandth power)}$$

What about a nation of "I's"/eyes?

> *For as we have many members in one body, and all members have not the same office: So we, being many, are one body in Christ, and every one members one of another* ***(Romans 12:4-5)****.*

Look at Jesus, like Father, like Son:

Father ←— II —→ Son

(Roman Numeral 2)

But to us there is but one God, the Father, of whom are all things, and we in him; and one Lord Jesus Christ, by whom are all things, and we by him ***(1 Corinthians 8:6)****. I and my Father are one* ***(John 10:30)****.*

God is One, and Jesus is One. They are two (2) I's/eyes looking upon us. Does a water's image change their appearance?

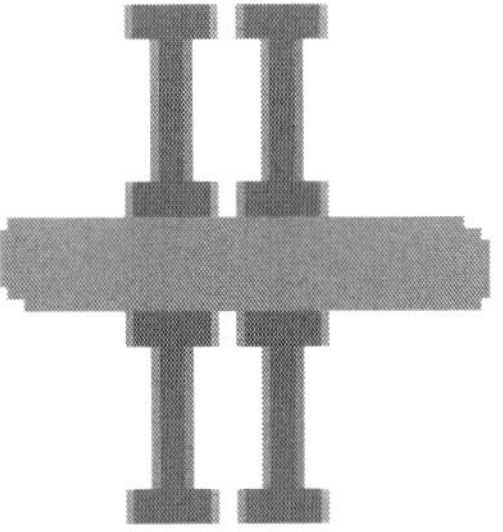

Jesus Christ the same yesterday, and to day, and for ever ***(Hebrews 13:8)****.*

Going a step further, the Father, Son, and Holy Ghost are three.

(Roman Numeral 3)

In the see/sea of water, as a roman numeral, aren't they the same?

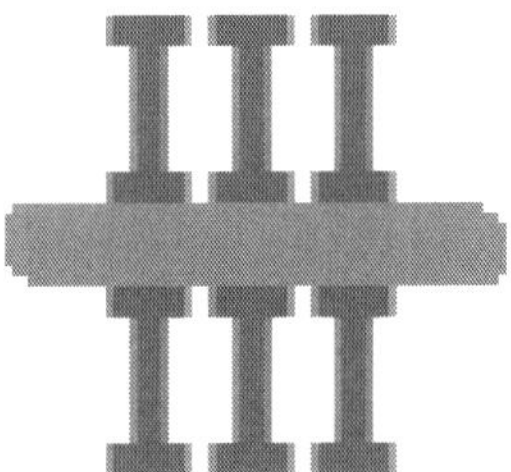

For there are three that bear record in heaven, the Father, the Word, and the Holy Ghost: and these three are one. And there are three that bear witness in earth,

> *the Spirit, and the water, and the blood: and these three agree in one* ***(1 John 5:7-8)****.*

From a water's reflection, it shows that JESUS reason's with us:

> *Come now, and let us reason together, saith the LORD: though your sins be as scarlet, they shall be as white as snow; though they be red like crimson, they shall be as wool* ***(Isaiah 1:18)****.*

Picking up where I left off, with the nation of "I's", this time, I will use "I" (roman numeral one), by multiplying "I" 3 times:

$$\mathrm{I} \times \mathrm{I} \times \mathrm{I} = \mathrm{I}^3 = \mathrm{I}$$

In the same likeness:

$$1 \times 1 \times 1 = 1^3 = 1$$

The points between them are to multiply our blessings, as they (the Father, Son, and Holy Ghost) come together as one. Isn't it amazing how mathematics doesn't have the power source to change the Father, Son, and Holy Ghost? Perhaps, it's because "They" are the highest power in one. They are also over all nations. But, if anyone of us were in the mix with the

Father, the Son, and the Holy Ghost, as a roman numeral, we are presented as:

(Roman Numeral 4)

Isn't something out of line? There seems to be conflict with two coming together. Aren't we bumping feet, and tripping on the Lord? We seem to be in disagreement. Perhaps, we are roman/roaming around, creating our own paths. What happened to the straight path that we are supposed to walk in? Look at roman numeral four (IV) under water:

It shows that we are bumping heads with the Lord. Perhaps, that's the reason that a person can start tripping, and bump heads all at the same time. That God created the waters, as He created a sea/see, how do you sea/see yourself in the image of water?

> *And God saw that the wickedness of man was great in the earth, and that every imagination of the thoughts of his heart was only evil continually. And it repented the LORD that he had made man on the earth, and it grieved him at his heart. And the LORD said, I will destroy man whom I have created from the face of the earth; both man, and beast, and the creeping thing, and the fowls of the air; for it repenteth me that I have made them* ***(Genesis 6:5-7)***.

Aren't we upside down?

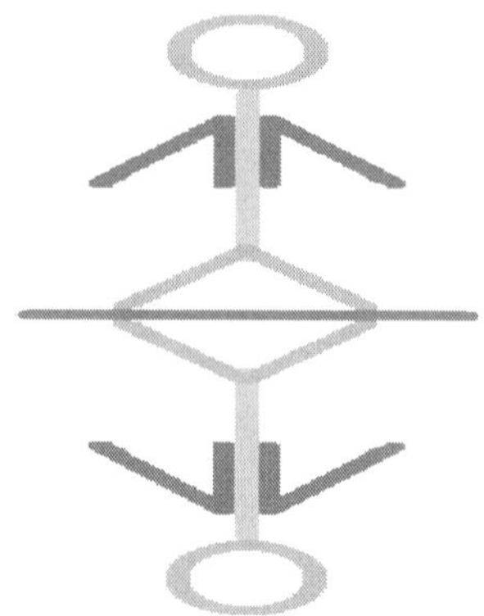

Again, doesn't water reveal truth? As man is poor/poured without the wisdom of God, we are as a glass turned upside down leaking tears of sadness. Therefore, without the guidance of the Lord, our knowledge is as an empty glass.

> *Behold, the LORD maketh the earth empty, and maketh it waste, and turneth it upside down, and scattereth abroad the inhabitants thereof. The land shall be utterly emptied, and utterly spoiled: for the LORD hath spoken this word. The earth mourneth and fadeth away, the world languisheth and fadeth away, the haughty people of the earth do languish. The earth also is defiled under the inhabitants thereof; because they have transgressed the laws, changed the ordinance, broken the everlasting covenant* ***(Isaiah 24:1, and 3-5)****. Surely your turning of things upside down shall be esteemed as the potter's clay: for shall the work say of him that made it, He made me not? or shall the thing framed say of him that framed it, He had no understanding* ***(Isaiah 29:16)****?*

But, by the counsel of God, we can be turned right side up and stay filled through the richness of His word, as He pours into us, joy and blessings. Isn't it amazing how the Lord uses reverse sea-chology (reverse psychology) to reveal truth? No matter what number of I's (the letter) that we power up to, as a nation, our power will never reach the highest margin of the Lord's.

> *And it shall come to pass afterward, that I will pour out my spirit upon all flesh; and your sons and your daughters shall prophesy, your old men shall dream dreams, your young men shall see visions: And also upon the servants and upon the handmaids in those days will I pour out my spirit* ***(Joel 2:28-29)***.

If "WE" work together, as a team, then "WE" can stand on top of water. But, if "WE" were under water, the reflection of water would reveal "WE" as a "ME".

"ME" would drown by myself. "ME" would also waiver, as the waves of the water. Water speaks truth, because it's clear. You see, "WE" have 2 letters, and 2 or more makes a team. "ME" also have 2 letters, but that's "ME" hanging in there by ME-self. Now, does that make "ME" true to myself? Actually, "ME"

hanging underwater by myself and surviving without a team, ha, something's fishy about that.

Perhaps, "ME" by myself, underwater, will be well deserted/deserved. Therefore, "ME" would be a great dessert to the Well family of sharks and crocodiles. Underwater, without a team, "ME" would never make it. "ME" would be well eaten alive.

"A DESERTED ISLAND THAT MAY HAVE YOU AS A DESSERT THAT IS 'WELL' APPRECIATED, AND SPEAKS VOLUMES TO THE SHARKS AND CROCODILES"

*Now the LORD had prepared a great fish to swallow up Jonah. And Jonah was in the belly of the fish three days and three nights **(Jonah 1:17)**.*

On the flipside, if "ME" was into "ME"-self or "WE" was into "WE"-selves (ourselves), that's putting your beliefs in you and perhaps, your teammates, but not seeking God's trust, then "ME" and "WE" would come together as a fence/de-fense towards each other, through our own minds. Hence, "WE" and "ME" coming together, as a team, without Jehovah, will form our own prison gates, being in the state of confusion:

"M" AND "W" COMING TOGETHER AS A FENCED ELECTRIC PRISON GATE

In other words, not looking to God, in all that we do, will put us in a confused state of mind, as we will put the blame on others.

If you are only about "Me, Myself and I", then how far will you get in life? But, if you let God be your I/eye, to takeover, your daily routine will turnout much better than a "C"/see, as HE works it out through you, then you will upgrade to an A-men.

God is also referred to as "HE". When "HE" connects with "HE"-self from a water's reflection, "HE" is still "HE". Furthermore, "HE" divided by His reflection is 1, which turns to GOD being, also, 1:

HE / HE becomes - HE -

But, our reflection of "WE" and "ME" will change when "WE" and "ME" connect. Therefore, we are something else. That's why we have to watch what we reflect upon.

If you are good, wouldn't you be seen as good in the scene of water?

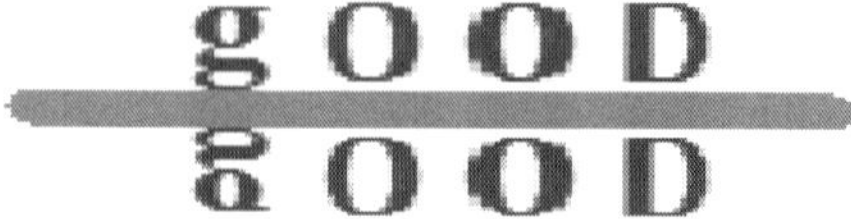

Moreover, if God was in a sea/see of water, does God change?

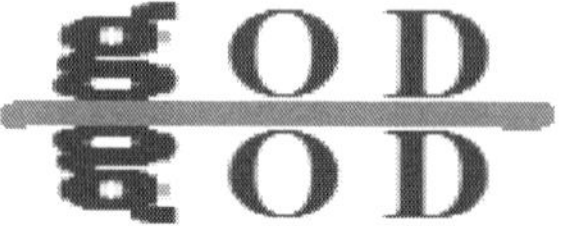

> *For I am the LORD, I change not; therefore ye sons of Jacob are not consumed* ***(Malachi 3:6)****.*

Let's look at our "LIFE" from a mirror's perspective:

LIFE | ƎᖷI⅃

Do you see life as an "E-file"? But, man made the mirror. Therefore, looking from a man's perspective, "LIFE" does not seem to be rite/right. If an e-file is bad instead of showing life, then how are you revealed from a mirror's perspective, if you were bad?

bAd | bAd

The fool hath said in his heart, There is no God. They are corrupt, they have done abominable works, there is none that doeth good ***(Psalm 14:1)****. There is a way which seemeth right unto a man, but the end thereof are the ways of death* ***(Proverbs 14:12)****. Every way of a man is right in his own eyes: but the LORD pondereth the hearts* ***(Proverbs 21:2)****.*

It looks like, coming from man's perspective, you will do bAd for bAd. God's will is not for us to turn bAd around for bAd. If you do not change the bAd, bAd will only repeat itself, until you change for the better.

> *And be not conformed to this world: but be ye transformed by the renewing of your mind, that ye may prove what is that good, and acceptable, and perfect, will of God* ***(Romans 12:2)****. Woe unto them that seek deep to hide their counsel from the LORD, and their works are in the dark, and they say, Who seeth us? and who knoweth us* ***(Isaiah 29:15)****?*

Speaking about "bAd", if the devil looked himself in the mirror, how would he see himself?

devil | liveb

IT LOOKS LIKE THE DEVIL WILL LIVE BACKWARDS BASED ON THE WORD OF GOD, AS THE "B" (IN THE MIRROR) STANDS FOR "BACKWARD". ALSO, DOING-EVIL (DEVIL) IS LIVING BACKWARDS

> *A prudent man foreseeth the evil, and hideth himself: but the simple pass on, and are punished* ***(Proverbs 22:3)****.*

Isn't it something how everything that is emitted in time has a spell on it? The things that we do, say, and think are manifested in our lives. Therefore, we have to be careful what we emit, because it turns back in time.

emit spelled backward is time.

Likewise, coming from a mirror's perspective, "emit" on the other side of the cell is doing "time":

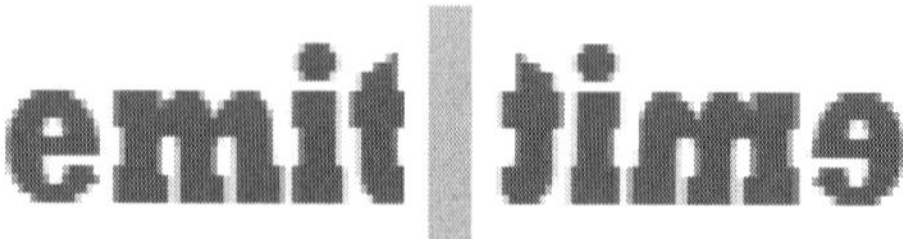

> *But all things that are reproved are made manifest by the light: for whatsoever doth make manifest is light* ***(Ephesians 5:13)****.*

But, if we want to turn things around in time, for our lives, we have to emit the good, and not the bad. Furthermore, God just want a mite portion of our time, so that He can work mightily for us. Our time for God, should have no limit. Therefore, there shall be no time line for God.

limit spelled backward is **timil.**

tim x (i) x (l) =
tim (li) =
tim line = time line

Therefore, coming from a mirror's perspective, a "limit" faces a "timeline":

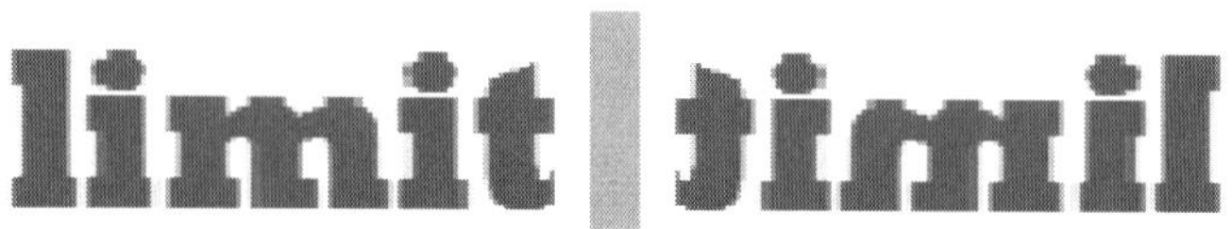

If you look at the Father, Son, and Holy Ghost (as a roman numeral 3), from a mirror's perspective, will they change?

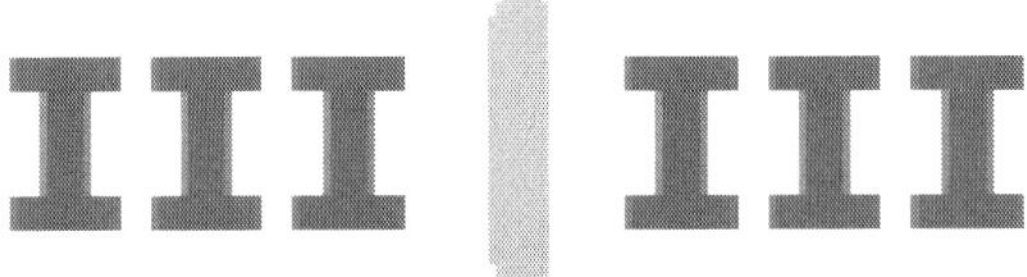

But, if we look at ourselves to be added in with the Father, Son, and Holy Ghost, as a roman numeral, don't we turn things around?

IV VI

> *For none of us liveth to himself, and no man dieth to himself. For whether we live, we live unto the Lord; and whether we die, we die unto the Lord: whether we live therefore, or die, we are the Lord's* ***(Romans 14:7-8)****.*

Roman numeral 4 (IV) is revealed in a mirror's image as a roman numeral 6 (VI). As we are all associated as man in the bible, doesn't the number six (6) stand for man? Moreover, if "MAN" stands in the mirror, will he not see himself, for who he is, by name?

MAN ИAM

> *Neither is there salvation in any other: for there is none other name under heaven given among men, whereby we must be saved* ***(Acts 4:12)****. A good name is rather to be chosen than great riches, and loving favour rather than silver and gold* ***(Proverbs 22:1)****.*

Everything in life has a purpose. In all things that we do, God already knew that it was going to happen, and everything that exist has a name on it. Therefore, every name is spelled with its own unique purpose.

> *In whom also we have obtained an inheritance, being predestinated according to the purpose of him who worketh all things after the counsel of his own will: That we should be to the praise of his glory, who first trusted in Christ* ***(Ephesians 1:11-12)****.*

If a roman numeral 4 (IV) was connected to itself, from a water's perspective, it would be seen as a roman numeral 9 (IX):

That the number 9 stands for divine completion, finality, and judgment, it looks like we would give ourselves complete attention. Therefore, if we, as a IV (roman numeral 4), tried to manipulate the spirit of the Father, Son, and Holy Ghost, a water's perspective will show each one of us coming to a dead-end, or to a final point in life.

> *He that believeth on me, as the scripture hath said, out of his belly shall flow rivers of living water* ***(John 7:38)****. (But this spake he of the Spirit, which they that believe on him should receive: for the Holy Ghost was not yet given; because that Jesus was not yet glorified* ***(John 7:39)****.) But whosoever drinketh of the water that I shall give him shall never thirst; but the water that I shall give him shall be in him a well of water springing up into everlasting life* ***(John 4:14)****.*

Also, as was stated earlier, if a roman numeral 4 (IV) looked itself in the mirror, it would see itself as man (roman numeral 6 = VI).

But, as the water and mirror perspectives collaborate, the roman numeral 4 (IV) is scened/seen as a roman numeral 9 (IX), and a roman numeral 11 (XI):

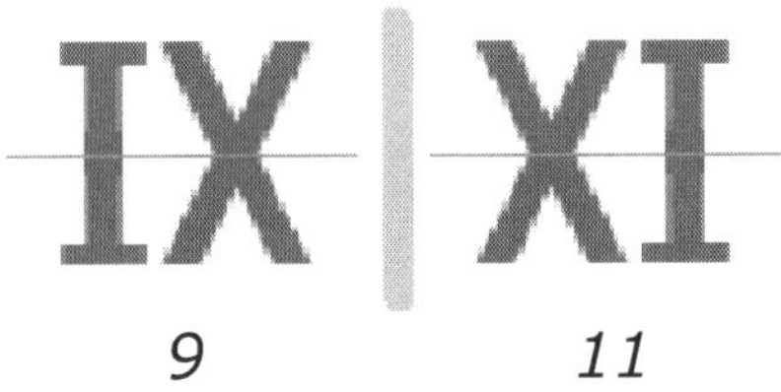

9 11

That sure/shore looks like an emergency call, observing the whole picture of ourselves, or observing ourselves as a whole number. God is the Doctor of all doctors. If we are under His care, doesn't that make each one of us His emergency?

> *But it shall come to pass, if thou wilt not hearken unto the voice of the LORD thy God, to observe to do all his commandments and his statutes which I command thee this day; that all these curses shall come upon thee, and overtake thee: Cursed shalt thou be in the city, and cursed shalt thou be in the field. Cursed shall be thy basket and thy store. Cursed shall be the fruit of thy body, and the fruit of thy land, the increase of thy kine, and the flocks of thy sheep. Cursed shalt thou be when thou comest in, and cursed shalt thou be when thou goest out* ***(Deuteronomy 28:15-19)****.*

Both of the numbers, 9 and 11 stands for judgment. Perhaps, that's why we have to look at ourselves, before judging someone else. Moreover, would you rather be puzzled with this world, or jointed to God's puzzle, and stay connected?

> *And I saw the dead, small and great, stand before God; and the books were opened: and another book was opened, which is the book of life: and the dead were judged out of those things which were written in the books, according to their works. And the sea gave up the dead which were in it; and death and hell delivered up the dead which were in them: and they were judged every man according to their works. And death and hell were cast into the lake of fire. This is the second death. And whosoever was not found written in the book of life was cast into the lake of fire* ***(Revelations 20:12-15)****.*

When we stay connected with God, it is by prayer and His grace upon us. The number 5 stands for grace. If this number is shown as a roman numeral, it would be presented as "V". When two people come together for prayer in Jesus' name, and the prayer in which they are praying is in God's will, God will have grace upon them.

CAn yoU ReAD between THe LINes?

> *Wherefore we receiving a kingdom which cannot be moved, let us have grace, whereby we may serve God acceptably with reverence and godly fear: For our God is a consuming fire* ***(Hebrews 12:28-29)****. As ye have therefore received Christ Jesus the Lord, so walk ye in*

> *him: Rooted and built up in him, and stablished in the faith, as ye have been taught, abounding therein with thanksgiving* ***(Colossians 2:6-7)***.

If you put your hand to a mirror, as 5 stands for grace, what collaboration does a mirror's image present when you put your hand to a test of glass?

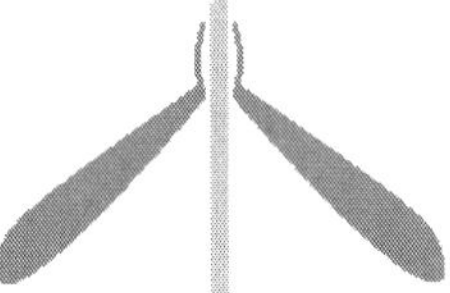

Doesn't your hand and the reflection of your hand come together for grace and prayer? Perhaps, when we have grace through God, He deserves a high-five.

> *Praying always with all prayer and supplication in the Spirit, and watching thereunto with all perseverance and supplication for all saints* ***(Ephesians 6:18)***;

Let's do a mirror and water collaboration demonstration:

Doesn't it come together as a diamond? I call this my collaboration diamond-stration, instead of a demonstration. It removes the demon from the source, through grace. A diamond is a precious gem.

Isn't prayer and grace also a precious exercise for our everyday workout? It will make you stronger, sharper, brighter, and give you great cuts, especially when we connect as a workout through prayer, in a gem/gym.

> *Happy is the man that findeth wisdom, and the man that getteth understanding. For the merchandise of it is better than the merchandise of silver, and the gain thereof than fine gold. She is more precious than rubies: and all the things thou canst desire are not to be compared unto her* ***(Proverbs 3:13-15)****. The LORD by wisdom hath founded the earth; by understanding hath he established the heavens. By his knowledge the depths are broken up, and the clouds drop down the dew. My son, let not them depart from thine eyes: keep sound wisdom and discretion: So shall they be life unto thy soul, and grace to thy neck* ***(Proverbs 3:19-22)****.*

A mirror's image can not change an agreement in prayer. Neither can a mirror's image change a roman numeral 5 (V) to tell/tale/tail a different story.

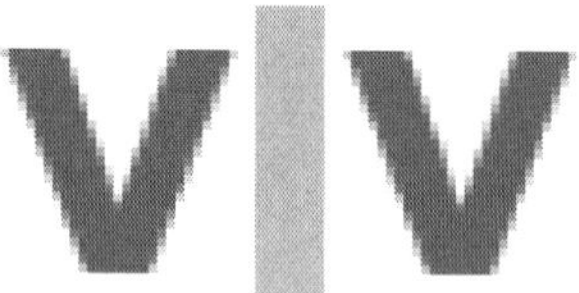

> *To all that be in Rome, beloved of God, called to be saints: Grace to you and peace from God our Father, and the Lord Jesus Christ* ***(Romans 1:7)****.*

Grace, that God gives us, will still be grace from a mirror's perspective. But, from a mirror's and water's reflection, when the roman numeral 5 (V) is connected to itself, it Pacifically (specifically) seas/sees as a roman numeral 10 (X) from both sides of the mirror:

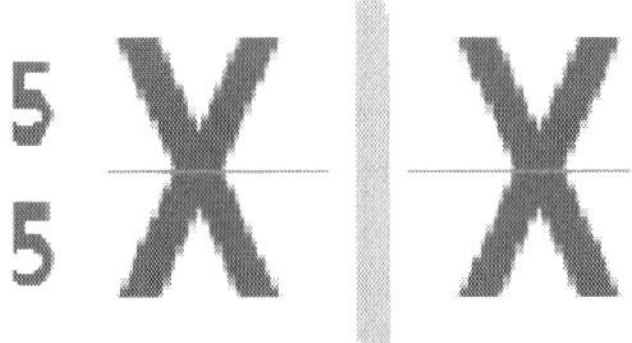

That 5 + 5 is 10, isn't grace also true?

> *And the Word was made flesh, and dwelt among us, (and we beheld his glory, the glory as of the only begotten of the Father,) full of grace and truth. And of his fulness have all we received, and grace for grace* ***(John 1:14 and 16)****.*

But, when we are stuck on ourselves, all things do not add up correctly:

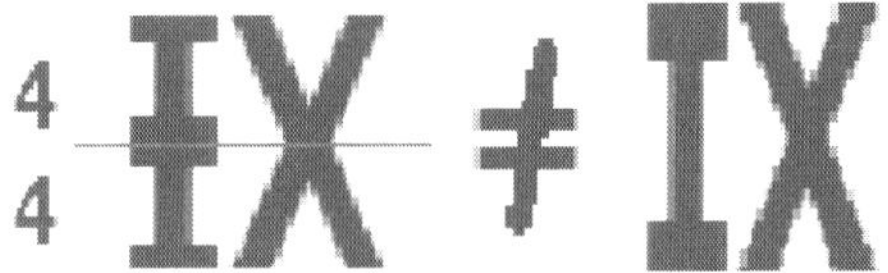

4 + 4 does not equal to 9.

> *Then the LORD said unto me, The prophets prophesy lies in my name: I sent them not, neither have I commanded them, neither spake unto them: they prophesy unto you a false vision and divination, and a thing of nought, and the deceit of their heart* ***(Jeremiah 14:14)****.*

In another scenario: If there is division between to parties, the aftermath of the problem will not add up to the same, in agreement. Instead, it may be an argument.

$$\frac{\text{PARTY1}}{\text{PARTY2}} \neq \text{PARTY1} + \text{PARTY2}$$

PARTY1 ÷ PARTY2 ≠ PARTY1 + PARTY2.
WORKING IN DIVISION ≠ WORKING AS A TEAM.

> *And Jesus knew their thoughts, and said unto them, Every kingdom divided against itself is brought to desolation; and every city or house divided against itself shall not stand: And if Satan cast out Satan, he is divided against himself; how shall then his kingdom stand **(Matthew 12:25-26)**?*

The number 10 stands for perfection and completion. Without grace (V), our lives cannot be complete, and neither can we show a reflection upon perfection:

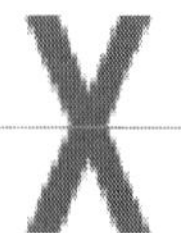

Moreover, when the grace of praise goes up, then the blessings of grace comes down.

It has been said, "There are two sides to every story." Isn't it amazing how the Father, Son, and Holy Ghost, as a roman numeral 3 (III) image's stories doesn't change, but we do, when we are roman/roaming around, trying to fix things ourselves? If grace, from a mirror's perspective, does not change, and neither does perfection, then why not trust in God to make your life complete?

> *Trust in the LORD with all thine heart; and lean not unto thine own understanding. In all thy ways acknowledge him, and he shall direct thy path **(Proverbs 3:5-6)**. The LORD preserveth the strangers; he relieveth the fatherless and widow: but the way of the wicked he turneth upside down **(Psalm 146:9)**.*

PART 2:

ON-BRAND PLAY ON WORDS QUOTES AND POETRY

"If 'U' Were Upside Down"

If "u" were upside down, "u" would come to an "n" (end), which could come to "nothing." Therefore, God's creation is for "u" to stand for something.

If the Lord knocks and we don't answer, we can't blame it on the ...BEL (bell). We would "JEZ" (just) miss our calling. There's nothing "EZ" (easy) about that, because if we have no true guidance in our walk of life, then we will "J-walk" (jaywalk) and get runover. A "J-walk is as dangerous as cutting a "U-turn" short. Doesn't it look like "JEZEBEL" written all around this scenario?

> *And there was none like unto Ahab, which did sell himself to work wickedness in the sight of the LORD, whom Jez'-e-bel his wife stirred up* ***(1 Kings 21:25)****. And Jez'-e-bel his wife said unto him, Dost thou govern the kingdom of Israel? Arise, and eat bread, and let thine heart be merry: I will give thee the vineyard of Na'-both the Jez'-re-el-ite. So she wrote letters in Ahab's name, and sealed them with his seal, and sent the letters unto the elders and to the nobles that were in his city, dwelling with Na'-both. And she wrote in the letters, saying, Proclaim a fast, and set Na'-both on high among*

> *the people: And set two men, sons of Be'-li-al, before him, to bear witness against him, saying, Thou didst blaspheme God and the king. And then carry him out, and stone him, that he may die* ***(1 Kings 21:7-10)***.

Now, let's put "i" in the place of "u": If "i" were upside down, "i" would become an exclamation point (!). Look at the dot as a person's head, and the line as the body.

If "i" were upside down for too long, "i" would become a question mark (?), like a loss of balance.

People would wonder as wonders with questions. Therefore, "i" stand for something. If you let people turn you around, then you will come to noT.

you noʎ

If "you" turned short of operating in a full circle, of God's guidance, through life, wouldn't "you" turn to "noT"? A full circle is 360 degrees, as a half circle is 180 degrees. God doesn't want "you" to operate in only half of His circle. He wants "you" to operate in His full circle, so when it becomes your turn for your blessings, God wants to give you the whole pizza (piece of) works.

Furthermore, if you were turned into a **KnoT/noT**, would you get a loose from bondage?

I'M TIED UP AT THE MOMENT.

> *Therefore, my beloved brethren, be ye stedfast, unmoveable, always abounding in the work of the Lord, forasmuch as ye know that your labour is not in vain in the Lord* ***(1 Corinthians 15:58)****.*

"From Hopscotch To Plain Old Scotch"

It's something how the activities of many children have changed. They used to have a great time playing "Hopscotch." These days, they leave out the hopping and go straight for the Scotch.

GIRL JUMPING HOPSCOTCH

BOY LEAVES OUT THE HOP AND GOES STRAIGH T FOR THE SCOTCH

> *Train up a child in the way he should go: and when he is old, he will not depart from it* ***(Proverbs 22:6)****.*

"Never Miss A Hit Through God's Will"

The Lord's will/wheel is true. Therefore, by His will/wheel we will drive for perfection to never miss a strike through His guidance, because the Lord keeps us in line. Therefore, we can hit a line drive every time, for no chance of sticking with a foul.

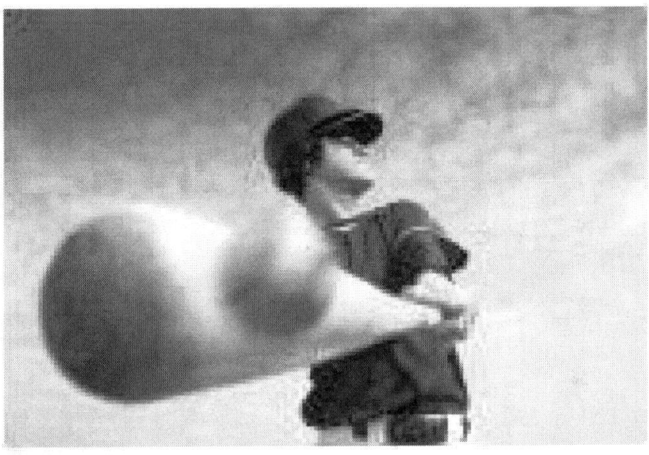

He is the Rock, his work is perfect: for all his ways are judgment: a God of truth and without iniquity, just and right is he ***(Deuteronomy 32:4)****. Trust in the LORD with all thine heart; and lean not unto thine own understanding. In all thy ways acknowledge him, and he shall direct thy paths* ***(Proverbs 3:5-6)****. And be not conformed to this world: but be ye transformed by the renewing of your mind, that ye may prove what is that good, and acceptable, and perfect, will of God* ***(Romans 12:2)****. Be ye therefore perfect, even as your Father which is in heaven is perfect* ***(Matthew 5:48)****.*

"Be Patient With Dr. God"

God is our Spiritual Doctor, so we are His patients. Therefore, He wants us to be patient with Him, during His time of healing.

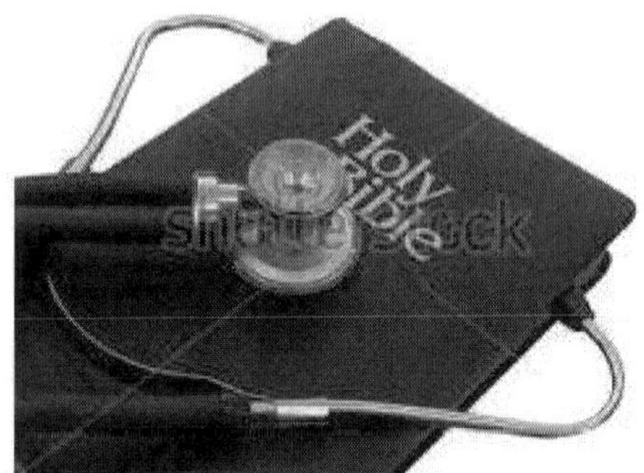

"Dr. God's Word's Of Wisdom With The Power To Heal"

And Jesus went about all Galilee, teaching in their synagogues, and preaching the gospel of the kingdom, and healing all manner of sickness and all manner of disease among the people. And his fame went throughout all Syria: and they brought unto him all sick people that were taken with divers diseases and torments, and those which were possessed with devils, and those which were lunatick, and those that had the palsy; and he healed them ***(Matthew 4:23-24)****. Then shall thy light break forth as the morning, and thine health shall spring forth speedily: and thy righteousness shall go before thee; the glory of the LORD shall be thy rereward* ***(Isaiah 58:8)****. But they that wait upon the LORD shall renew their strength; they shall mount up with wings as eagles; they shall run, and not be weary; and they shall walk, and not faint* ***(Isaiah 40:31)****.*

"Let Go and Let God"

Let "Go" and let "God", but don't let go of God, because without God you have nowhere to "Go".

> *Cast thy burden upon the LORD, and he shall sustain thee: he shall never suffer the righteous to be moved* ***(Psalm 55:22)****. Saying, Father, if thou be willing, remove this cup from me: nevertheless not my will, but thine, be done* ***(Luke 22:42)****. Whither shall I go from thy spirit? or whither shall I flee from thy presence? If I ascend up into heaven, thou art there: if I make my bed in hell, behold, thou art there. If I take the wings of the morning, and dwell in the uttermost parts of the sea; Even there shall thy hand lead me, and thy right hand shall hold me. If I say, Surely the darkness shall cover me; even the night shall be light about me. Yea, the darkness hideth not from thee; but the night shineth as the day: the darkness and the light are both alike to thee* ***(Psalms 139:7-12)****.*

"Chef Lord Of The Year"

It is said, "Taste and see that the Lord is good." He is seasoned all year around.

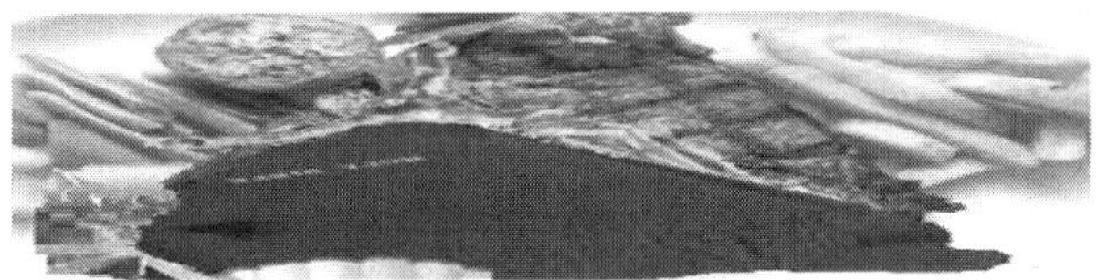

"GOD'S WORD IS AT STAKE/STEAK!"

Now, that's broken down to a "T", or shall I say, "...broken down to the 'Bone'?"

> *How sweet are thy words unto my taste! yea, sweeter than honey to my mouth* ***(Psalm 119:103)****.*

"God Created The Stars/Starrs"

Why is it that we are so excited to get in line to see a starr perform his/her act,

but we are so slow to stand in line for God's act, in our lives, who is the creator of all stars/all starrs/All-Stars?

Thou shalt have no other gods before me. Thou shalt not make unto thee any graven image, or any likeness

of any thing that is in heaven above, or that is in the earth beneath, or that is in the water under the earth. Thou shalt not bow down thyself to them, nor serve them: for I the LORD thy God am a jealous God, visiting the iniquity of the fathers upon the children unto the third and fourth generation of them that hate me ***(Exodus 20:3-5)****. For by him were all things created, that are in heaven, and that are in earth, visible and invisible, whether they be thrones, or dominions, or principalities, or powers: all things were created by him, and for him: And he is before all things, and by him all things consist* ***(Colossians 1:16-17)****.*

"God's Signs & Wonders vs Man's Signs & Wonders"

Here on earth, most houses have signs for an address, so you don't have to wonder and get lost. But, in God's house, there are many signs and wonders to be addressed so that you won't be lost.

And these signs shall follow them that believe; In my name shall they cast out devils; they shall speak with new tongues; They shall take up serpents; and if they drink any deadly thing, it shall not hurt them; they shall lay hands on the sick, and they shall recover ***(Mark 16:17-18).*** *God also bearing them witness, both with signs and wonders, and with divers miracles, and gifts of the Holy Ghost, according to his own will* ***(Hebrews 2:4).*** *The Lord is not slack concerning his promise, as some men count slackness; but is longsuffering to us-ward, not willing that any should perish, but that all should come to repentance* ***(2 Peter 3:9).*** *For this shall every one that is godly pray unto thee in a time*

> *when thou mayest be found: surely in the floods of great waters they shall not come nigh unto him* ***(Psalm 32:6).*** *And be found in him, not having mine own righteousness, which is of the law, but that which is through the faith of Christ, the righteousness which is of God by faith* ***(Philippians 3:9).*** *Wherefore, beloved, seeing that ye look for such things, be diligent that ye may be found of him in peace, without spot, and blameless* ***(2 Peter 3:14).***

"Instead Of 'God Forbid' We Should Bid For God"

So often, when we see or hear things that we don't want to deal with, we use the term "God forbid!" On the flipside, when we go through different trials and tribulations in life, we should Bid For God.

> *Trust in the LORD with all thine heart; and lean not unto thine own understanding. In all thy ways acknowledge him, and he shall direct thy paths. Be not wise in thine own eyes: fear the LORD, and depart from evil. It shall be health to thy navel, and marrow to thy bones* ***(Proverbs 3:5-8)****. These things I have spoken unto you, that in me ye might have peace. In the world ye shall have tribulation: but be of good cheer; I have overcome the world* ***(John 16:33)****.*

"Trust In God Who Is Over Time"

If we build up trust over time, shouldn't we trust in God who is <u>over time</u> and works <u>overtime</u> (OT)?

> *Behold ye among the heathen, and regard, and wonder marvelously: for I will work a work in your days, which*

ye will not believe, though it be told you ***(Habakkuk 1:5)****. And he said unto them, It is not for you to know the times or the seasons, which the Father hath put in his own power* ***(Acts 1:7)****. I must work the works of him that sent me, while it is day: the night cometh, when no man can work. As long as I am in the world, I am the light of the world* ***(John 9:4-5)****. Now unto him that is able to do exceeding abundantly above all that we ask or think, according to the power that worketh in us, unto him be glory in the church by Christ Jesus throughout all ages, world without end. A-men'* ***(Ephesians 3:20-21)****.*

"Don't Do Evil For Evil"

We should not do evil for evil. That will only brings about more evil. But, if someone does evil onto you, turn it around to live. That comes through fasting and praying.

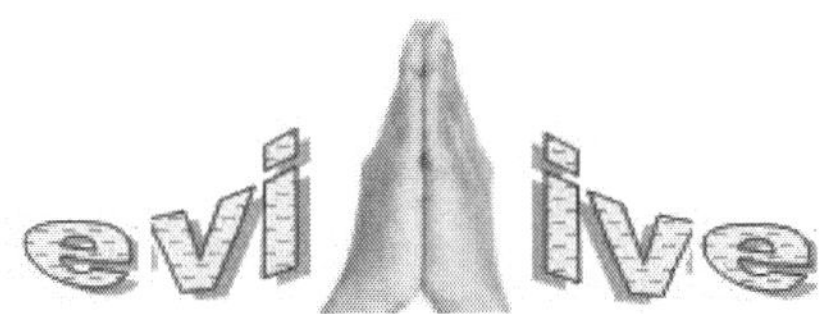

Moreover, if you turn "bAd" around for "bAd", it will still be "bAd".

turned around is still

That goes back to: negative (-) X negative (-), through Christ Jesus, does not turn things around for a positive.

> *Finally, be ye all of one mind, having compassion one of another, love as brethren, be pitiful, be courteous: Not rendering evil for evil, or railing for railing: but contrariwise blessing; knowing that ye are thereunto called, that ye should inherit a blessing. For HE THAT WILL LOVE LIFE, AND SEE GOOD DAYS, LET HIM REFRAIN HIS TONGUE FROM EVIL, AND HIS LIPS THAT THEY SPEAK NO GUILE: LET HIM ESCHEW EVIL, AND DO GOOD; LET HIM SEEK PEACE, AND ENSUE IT. FOR THE EYES OF THE LORD ARE OVER THE RIGHTOUS, AND HIS EARS ARE OPEN UNTO THEIR PRAYERS: BUT THE FACE OF THE LORD IS AGAINST THEM THAT DO EVIL* ***(I Peter 3:8-12)****.*

"God Will Merri-nade/Marinade Your Walk"

Don't marry a person by the way they walk, but your walk with God makes your relationship merry.

> *A merry heart maketh a cheerful countenance: but by sorrow of the heart the spirit is broken* ***(Proverbs 15:13)****. There is therefore now no condemnation to them which are in Christ Jesus, who walk not after the flesh, but after the spirit* ***(Romans 8:1)****.*

"A Suit In Court"

When you have a suit in court, shall you be suited for the judge, or should you come as you are for the suit against you, or the suit that you are in?

Both parties in house shall be tied up from the start, as the judge takes no sides. It supposed to be a clear sharp cut down the middle of the suit.

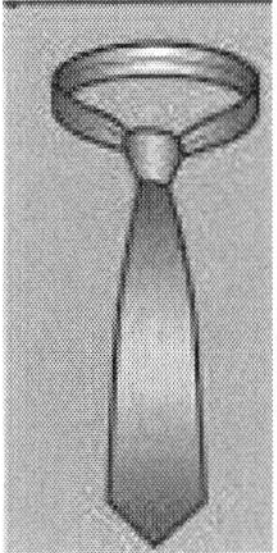

Why should the judge take suit on one side because of

what you "ADD DRESS TO"/"ADDRESS TO" your being an in-vest (investment)?

Is a suit that is a three piece better than a two piece,

THREE PIECE SUIT

TWO PIECE SUIT

or is the judge a-fraud (afraid) and opinionize to penalize/pen-a-lie, or pin-a-tie for one body over the other? What if one side had on a white button up dress shirt and the other side had on a blue button up dress shirt, does that make one side better than the other, because he was a "***White-collar***" vs a ***"Blue-collar"***?

There is a saying, "You shouldn't judge a book by its ***cover/color***." Well, a judge should not judge a body by its looks in a suit, but work by facts and not acts. How many people have been booked over what the situation looked like? It has also been said that a judge shall keep a track record of criminals. With that being said, if judges are supposed to have track records, then whom are they to judge? Isn't God our only judge that resides in heaven? Once again, when we go to God's house should we be suited and act our best, or come as we are?

> *But why dost thou judge thy brother? or why dost thou set at nought thy brother? for we shall all stand before the judgement seat of Christ. For it is written, AS I LIVE SAITH THE LORD, EVERY KNEE SHALL BOW TO ME, AND EVERY TONGUE SHALL CONFESS TO GOD. So then every one of us shall give account of himself to God* ***(Romans 14:10-12)***. *Judge not, that ye be not judged. For with what judgment ye judge, ye shall be judged: and with what measure ye mete, it shall be measured to you again. And why beholdest thou the mote that is in thy brother's eye, but considerest not the beam that is in thine own eye? Or how wilt thou say to thy brother, Let me pull out the mote out of thine eye; and, behold, a beam is in thine own eye? Thou hypocrite, first cast out the beam out of thine own eye; and then shalt see clearly to cast out the mote out of thy brother's eye* ***(Matthew 7:1-5)***. *For there is no respect of persons with God* ***(Romans 2:11)***.

"The Will/Wheel That Gives U Drive With No U-Turns"

U should treat the Bible as a car, because it gives U drive, through a steering will/wheel, without any U-turns. When Christ guides your drive, then He will take U out of any turns and steer U the right way, which is the straight way. Therefore, when ***Christ*** drives U ***Forward***, to take U straightaway, your path will always have the right way/right-of-way, as long as you are straight-up with Him.

For(war)d Christ(ler)

WHEN WE LET GOD WORK THROUGH OUR HANDS AND MINDS, THE ANOINTED PRODUCT WILL MAKE A NAME FOR ITSELF.

But be ye doers of the word, and not hearers only, deceiving your own selves. For if any be a hearer of the word, and not a doer, he is like unto a man beholding his natural face in a glass: For he beholdeth himself, and goeth his way, and straightway forgetteth what manner of man he was. But whoso looketh into the perfect law of liberty, and continueth therein, he being not a forgetful hearer, but a doer of the work, this man shall be blessed in his deed. If any man among you seem to be religious, and bridleth not his tongue, but deceiveth his own heart, this man's religion is vain ***(James 1:22-26)***.

"Knock On The Lord's Door"

Knock on the Lord's door and He will open up His shore, and that's a sure/shore thing. Knock on His door through prayer, and He will show you His care, because He will carry out His promise every time. But, can you flow with it?

WHEN YOU PUT YOUR TRUST IN GOD, HE WILL GIVE YOU AN OVERFLOW OF BLESSINGS.

Ask, and it shall be given you; seek, and ye shall find; knock, and it shall be opened unto you: For every one that asketh receiveth; and he that seeketh findeth; and to him that knocketh it shall be opened ***(Matthew 7:7-8)****. He that believeth on me, as the scripture hath said, out of his belly shall flow rivers of living water* ***(John 7:38)****.*

ABOUT THE AUTHOR

With the publication of Brandon T. Mitchell's fourth novel, He has many unique flowing thoughts that the Lord, God, births into his mind, day by day. As they become overwhelming, he wants to share his knowledge with others. Brandon T. Mitchell, at many times, was misunderstood, but his educational background proves him to be more advanced than what many individuals labeled him to be. He has a Bachelor's Degree from Tennessee State University in Family and Consumer Sciences with a Concentration in Interior Design, and a MBA in Accounting with a 4.0 GPA from Jones International University. Many downfalls in the past has only made Brandon T. Mitchell a stronger person in life. He is a fighter for what he believes, and never gives up on his dreams.

Made in the USA
Columbia, SC
10 September 2024